The Dolby era

D1574994

Published in our
centenary year
～ **2004** ～
MANCHESTER
UNIVERSITY
PRESS

Inside Popular Film

General editors Mark Jancovich and Eric Schaefer

Inside Popular Film is a forum for writers who are working to develop new ways of analysing popular film. Each book offers a critical introduction to existing debates while also exploring new approaches. In general, the books give historically informed accounts of popular film, which present this area as altogether more complex than is commonly suggested by established film theories.

Developments over the past decade have led to a broader understanding of film, which moves beyond the traditional oppositions between high and low culture, popular and avant-garde. The analysis of film has also moved beyond a concentration on the textual forms of films, to include an analysis of both the social situations within which films are consumed by audiences, and the relationship between film and other popular forms. The series therefore addresses issues such as the complex intertextual systems that link film, literature, art and music, as well as the production and consumption of film through a variety of hybrid media, including video, cable and satellite.

The authors take interdisciplinary approaches, which bring together a variety of theoretical and critical debates that have developed in film, media and cultural studies. They neither embrace nor condemn popular film, but explore specific forms and genres within the contexts of their production and consumption.

Already published:

The Dolby era

Film sound in contemporary Hollywood

Gianluca Sergi

Manchester University Press
Manchester and New York
distributed exclusively in the USA by Palgrave

Copyright © Gianluca Sergi 2004

The right of Gianluca Sergi to be identified as the author of this work has been asserted by him in accordance with the Copyright, Designs and Patens Act 1988.

Published by Manchester University Press
Oxford Road, Manchester M13 9NR, UK
and Room 400, 175 Fifth Avenue, New York, NY 10010, USA
www.manchesteruniversitypress.co.uk

Distributed exclusively in the USA by
Palgrave, 175 Fifth Avenue, New York,
NY 10010, USA

Distributed exclusively in Canada by
UBC Press, University of British Columbia, 2029 West Mall,
Vancouver, BC, Canada V6T 1Z2

British Library Cataloguing-in-Publication Data
A catalogue record for this book is available from the British Library

Library of Congress Cataloging-in-Publication Data applied for

ISBN   0 7190 7066 X *hardback*
EAN   978 0 7190 7066 2
ISBN   0 7190 7067 8 *paperback*
EAN   978 0 7190 7067 9

First published 2004

13 12 11 10 09 08 07 06 05 04   10 9 8 7 6 5 4 3 2 1

Typeset in Sabon with Frutiger
by Northern Phototypesetting Co. Ltd, Bolton

Printed in Great Britain
by Bell & Bain Ltd, Glasgow

Contents

Illustrations

Acknowledgements

As I write these few words to thank the people who have helped me during the researching and writing of this book I realise how my acknowledgements can only scratch the surface. I apologise to all those whom I have forgotten to mention!

I am indebted to all my former colleagues at Staffordshire University and all my present ones at the University of Nottingham. Their constant practical and intellectual support has been essential to making this project possible.

To my very good friend and colleague Alan Lovell I owe more than I can possibly say in a few words. Thanks for being the first person to believe in this project!

I would like to thank Steve Neale, Richard Maltby, Peter Kramer, Rick Altman, Christine Gledhill and Mark Jancovich for the guidance and support they have provided whilst working on this project. It has been a privilege to be able to share thoughts and ideas with you all. Thanks also to Jacqui Clay whose typing expertise came to the rescue at a crucial time! I am very grateful to Sara Peacock for her incisive comments and supportive attitude as copy editor.

To my very good friends Kris Grainger, Nick Hayes, Sharon Burton, Loredana Germanó and, last but by no means least, Nigel Collier: very many thanks for keeping me sane throughout this project with your friendship!

Many thanks to Karen Atherton, Tom Bruchs, Mike Smith and Bill Wray at Dolby Laboratories for their kindness and help. Very special thanks to Ray Dolby and Ioan Allen for being such good hosts and for sparing some of the little free time they have to talk to me.

Many thanks also to Bruce Stambler and all those who had to bear with my questions at Soundstorm. Similarly I am thankful to Tomlinson Holman and the staff at TMH.

Very special thanks to Larry Blake for being such a constant source of material and ideas (and for travelling a few thousand miles to the UK to attend the Sounding Out conference!).

Many thanks to all at Skywalker Ranch. In particular I am indebted to Randy Thom for making himself available on different occasions and for his

insightful remarks. Very special thanks to Gary Rydstrom, who has had to
endure my persistence more than anyone else! I sincerely appreciate all our
conversations about sound, be they across a dinner table or across an ocean.
It has been a real pleasure and an education.

Very extra special thanks to all sound men and women out there whose
work I have admired over the years. Keep the good sound coming!

Finally, I would like to thank my family, both in Italy and the UK. Without
your love, support, and never-failing patience none of this would have been
possible. Grazie a mia madre, a mio padre e a mio fratello Marcello!

I wish to dedicate this book and any good that may come out of it to my
wife Cathy and my daughter Monica. You are my guiding lights and a
source of constant joy. Thank you for everything!

Part I

Film sound in the Dolby era

Introduction: sound matters

It is only shallow people who do not judge by appearances. The mystery of the world is the visible, not the invisible. (Oscar Wilde)[1]

Sound matters. The simplicity of this brief statement could be deceiving. Few sentences hold as much potential to reveal the inner workings of the cinema industry as this short and apparently obvious assertion. This is true for all facets of cinema: from filmmaking to audience reception, from scholarly research to student learning; all aspects that characterise, shape and structure our understanding of cinema are directly evoked by that simple address, sound matters. Nor has sound mattered more than it does in contemporary cinema: the profound changes that have taken place in mainstream cinema since the arrival of Dolby technologies in the early 1970s are so pervasive as to make it possible to suggest that they ushered in a new 'era' of cinema. My study aims at exploring these changes and their implications within what I will call the Dolby era, an era that has its roots in the cultural and political movements of the 1960s, exploded in all its novelty and excitement in the 1970s, and matured beyond expectations over the following two decades.

My particular concern is to provide a first substantial account of sound in contemporary Hollywood cinema. Historically the understanding and appreciation of cinema in all its aspects, including scholarly research, have been shaped by a strong bias towards the image. As a direct consequence of this bias film sound has received comparatively little attention. This has left a substantial void: we know very little about how sound works in the cinema, especially in contemporary terms. Audiences around the world listen to, as well as look at, a movie; sound technology impacts on the way films are made and received as much as image technology; the soundtrack is an area of creativity as fertile and exciting as any in filmmaking, yet the majority of scholars and critics have by and large remained impervious to all things sound for nearly a century. The origin of this neglect can be traced to another short statement: film is a visual medium. The view these few words express seems relatively unproblematic for there is much evidence to support it. The vast majority of established theories and notions of cinema revolve around this statement, and so do the methods of analysis that scholars employ to investigate movies. Textual analysis, *mise-en-scène*, the auteur theory, views of spectatorship and audience behaviour, notions of genre, studies of performance, histories of the cinema, and issues of representation: these are but a handful of core concepts in film studies that operate from the assumption that film is indeed a visual medium. University courses underwrite this view: a quick survey of film and cinema studies syllabi will reveal a consistent and coherent sharing of themes and concerns most of which are structured around the understanding of film as a visual medium, just as 'visual literacy' is often invoked as a prerequisite for the successful film student. Books that announce themselves as 'an introduction to film' use film's visual ontology as a conceptual thread and their material is often arranged accordingly.[2] Film critics also routinely confirm this notion by employing expressions such as 'visually arresting', a 'must-see' movie and by focusing their reviews mostly around visual performance. Perhaps the most important confirmation of the veracity of the notion of film as a visual medium comes from the vocabulary that we all use to talk about the movies. We go and 'see' a film, we extol the virtues of 'visionary' directors, and most of our terminology of cinema revolves around the image (one example above all, the choice of terms we have to describe a shot: pan, crane, tracking, point of view, establishing, close-up, long, medium, etc.). Put bluntly, any attempt to study sound in the cinema must deal with the uncomfortable truth that the widely held assumption that film is a visual medium carries a related postulation: sound matters less than the image. In many ways, the urgency and *raison d'être* of this study is to begin to redress the balance.

In this sense, it might be wise to take nothing for granted and begin by asking some 'basic' questions that are central to this study: what is sound, what is Dolby, and why concentrate on contemporary Hollywood? The latter is perhaps the least problematic question to answer. I have chosen to focus on contemporary Hollywood cinema because it offers a dominant model of filmmaking and has been the cradle of all major developments in sound aesthetics and technology, particularly in the period with which I am concerned. In many ways, contemporary sound is one of the leading Hollywood exports in technological, aesthetic and financial terms. Since the coming of sound in the late 1920s, the history of film sound has been firmly located within American industry.[3] The greatest beneficiaries in aesthetic and financial terms have been American filmmakers (Spielberg, Coppola, Scorsese, Lucas, Kaufman, etc.), and American companies have established a virtual domination of the world market insofar as sound technology is concerned. Thus there is little doubt that Hollywood ought to be identified as the home of contemporary sound in ways that neither television nor the music industry could ever claim to be. However, where is 'Hollywood' when it comes to sound? Despite the proliferation of dubbing stages across the world, most movies are still mixed in Hollywood.[4] As far as sound is concerned, Hollywood is not just a place in Los Angeles where studios are based and films are made. In geo-filmic sound terms, Hollywood is in Los Angeles, but it is also in New York, just as much as it is in San Francisco. Indeed, unlike film production, sound's largest power base is arguably set around the San Francisco Bay Area, not in Los Angeles. This is a relevant aspect for it links directly the development of new sound in the Dolby era with the generation of filmmakers that I mentioned above who moved to Northern California to 'escape' the modes of production of traditional 'LA-Hollywood'. Thus it would be unwise to talk of Hollywood sound as if it were a single entity. Nor would it be wise to assume that the term I have chosen to qualify the era I am about to investigate is in any way easier to dissect. What does the term Dolby refer to? Does it refer to Ray Dolby, founder and developer of the Dolby sound system? Does it refer to the company itself, Dolby Laboratories, one of the most successful technological enterprises to have emerged since the 1970s? Does it refer to the sound system itself that Ray Dolby developed and Dolby Labs produced and sold to millions of cinema and home theatres worldwide? In many ways, Dolby is none of the above things I mentioned: it is all of them and more. It does not begin in the 1970s nor are we 'after' it. It is one of the seismic events in the history of cinema, yet it is one of the least studied. It is one of most noticeable factors to have influenced the development of film aesthetics in the last quarter of cinema's first century, yet it is one of the least understood. It is one of the most successful companies in the world of entertainment, yet its founder and major creative force is little known outside the industry. In short, it is a remarkable story that begs to be told. All stories need boundaries, structures, and questions to solve. Mine have been chosen to tell the story of Dolby as the fascinating account of how sound took centre stage in Hollywood filmmaking and ushered in a whole host of new creative possibilities for both filmmakers and audiences alike. Indeed, if anything, the problems inherent to the term Dolby itself are a reminder of how wide ranging the impact Dolby has had on the film industry actually is. It is in this inclusive sense of 'era' that the term Dolby is to be understood in this study.

Finally, the most difficult of those 'simple' questions remains: how to define sound. Film sound shares the same physical medium as music: that is, sound waves. This 'closeness' has often meant that the main critical vocabulary employed to analyse soundtracks would seem to have begged, borrowed and stolen from its music counterpart. This is particularly evident in the insistence on terms such as timbre, pitch, tone, which though evidently relevant are not flexible enough to articulate the complexity of contemporary soundtracks. Most noticeably, vocabularies of music are concerned with sound per se, whereas film sound works in a symbiosis with the image. This problem is emphasised by Rick Altman when he forcefully suggests that 'While all film sounds have loudness, pitch and timbre, not a single sound in cinema can be adequately described with musical terminology.'[5]

Thus, film scholars would seem to have borrowed a rather inadequate vocabulary, able to describe only a limited range of the complexity of a soundtrack. The consequence of this is a rather inadequate understanding of what a soundtrack actually is. Rather than being investigated as a combination of sound elements, the term 'soundtrack' has often come to signify only the film's music track, dialogue being firmly confined to the 'superior' realm of the screenwriter. This is a rather convenient way to arrange film perception and appreciation. By singling out particular elements of a soundtrack, critics have been able to praise individual achievers rather than focus on the much more complex issue of what actually becomes of these 'individual' achievements once they are recorded, mixed and reproduced not as single independent units, but as part of the complex structure that is a soundtrack. However, 'soundtrack' is a highly complex combination of four elements – effects, music, dialogue and silence – whose qualities are inextricably blended together to achieve a creative balance. Indeed, it is the relationship between these four elements that I regard as the core of the soundtrack.

To attempt to chart the development of the Dolby era is also to suggest a substantial move towards closer dialogue and integration between the world of academia and that of practitioners. Despite the availability of a rather large amount of interview material with sound men and women, mostly in either 'technical' journals or specialist Internet sites, traditionally there has been little attempt to integrate critical thinking with the more exquisitely practical aspects of film-making. Nevertheless, the potential for cooperation and debate has never been greater than in the period I am investigating. The rise of new figures in Hollywood sound and the increasing impact of sound on contemporary films have not yet won it the kind of prestige amongst filmmakers that other areas, such as cinematography and directing, have traditionally enjoyed. However, it is precisely because of this that filmmakers working in any of the different sound crafts are some of the most approachable professional figures in Holly-wood. The increase of new means of communication at the end of the twentieth century, the Internet in particular, has facilitated establish-ing and maintaining contacts with sound makers. In a study such as mine that purports to examine the impact of sound on contemporary Hollywood cinema, the issue of whether to establish contacts with the people I am to write about quickly becomes a rhetorical question. In this sense, the contacts that I have developed over the years during my research have been invaluable. Leading sound designers such as Gary Rydstrom (*Saving Private Ryan, Titanic, Jurassic Park* and *Ter-minator 2*), Bruce Stambler (*The Fugitive, Batman and Robin*, and *Clear and Present Danger*), Randy Thom (*Forrest Gump, Cast Away, Arlington Road*), and Tom Holman (inventor of the THX sound system, and former director of technology at Lucasfilm) are but a few examples of the filmmakers who have helped immensely with this project. Indeed, the degree to which I will be capable of integrating their views and experience in my writing should be a good measure of the success or otherwise of my project.

As with every book, the way material is structured means a great deal in terms of how it supports the author's key aims and its ultimate effectiveness. In my case, this is of particular relevance because of the aforementioned desire to encourage greater dialogue between scholars and practitioners. It is unusual, rather rare in fact, to find 'academic' books showing a substantial attempt at employing both traditional scholarly accounts and interviews. Examples of methodology to draw upon are therefore scarce. This poses several important questions: how to select, structure and harmonise disparate, though related, literary styles? How to deal with the figure and role of the scholar? What emphasis to place on the views and ideas of practitioners?

Since I wish economy of language and transparency to be guiding principles for my writing I have chosen to use only a relatively small number of the interviews that I carried out with practitioners. However, within that relatively small sample, I strive to allow those interviews to 'breathe' as freely as possible. In particular, I decided early on to limit as much as possible editorial intervention. This resulted in the choice to include interviews in their entirety rather than, as it is more traditional, extracting relevant passages from them. This is for two key reasons. I wish to provide readers with a precise sense of how the dialogue between scholars and film practitioners may develop. These two professional figures have not traditionally shared the same concerns or language. Thus, the 'journey' from being total strangers to engaging in free-flowing interaction is an integral and fundamental part in the process of establishing a successful relationship. In view of this, the second key reason for leaving interviews in their 'raw' format was to include the figure of the interviewer. Traditional accounts 'hide' the source questions, often for legitimate reasons. However, I found that my questions were as revealing of my attitudes towards sound (something that was crucial in forcing me to face my own sound preconceptions) as they were a conduit to further information, views and ideas. If anything, allowing myself into the book should alert all scholars with an interest in talking to practitioners about the difficulty of trying to manage and shape a lively exchange with filmmakers 'as it happens'. Invariably, my best-laid plans were thrown into question within the first few exchanges with my counterpart, if not even before the actual interview began.[6]

There is one important aspect that I have purposely left out of my account of sound in contemporary cinema. The contribution that home cinema has made to the rise of interest in film sound is unquestionable. This is true in terms of literature, technology and aesthetic awareness. However, it is precisely because of the size and scope of this area of film sound that I have decided not to discuss it other than incidentally. To include home cinema in my study in a meaningful manner would mean detracting attention from the core topic, the theatrical dimension of film sound. More importantly, several discussions with designers have convinced me that, though the two areas of theatrical cinema and home cinema are obviously related, filmmakers still 'make movies' for cinema release, not for home consumption. The scope, detail and intricacy of their films' soundtracks are not concerned with home reproduction. Indeed, several designers and supervising sound editors personally supervise the 'down-mix' of the film's soundtrack for home release.[7] In other words, given the control that audiences have on technical aspects such as volume, speakers placement and overall acoustics, and the actual existence in many cases of two (or more) distinct soundtracks, one for theatrical release and one for home video/DVD/Laserdisc, it is feasible to see the two as separate entities. The ways in which these two sound artefacts relate to each other is a subject undoubtedly worthy of proper investigation, but this is not the aim of my study.

Ultimately, the importance of my study resides less in the awareness that other scholars have constantly neglected sound and more in the realisation that it is important to learn more about sound. One of the major conceptual and intellectual obstacles to the development of a sustained scholarship of film sound can be traced back specifically to this issue: whenever scholars have written and talked about sound they have mostly done so as a reaction to the image bias that is so predominant in most film theory and history. Tom Levin argues that: 'The history of the development of cinema sound can be tread as an oscillation between its difference (from the image) understood as supplement and its difference understood as a threat'.[8]

This is perhaps inevitable, and my study is, at least in part, no exception. However, this is also another way in which sound can be further marginalised with respect to the image: even when we talk about sound we do so as a reaction to what people write about the image rather than as a means to research the wealth of new areas that sound can disclose to the enterprising scholar. In this sense, the investigation of Dolby, the dialogue with creators of sound, and the analytical framework I will propose are all part of an attempt to reveal some of the unexplored potential that film sound holds for anyone with a serious interest in the cinema. Sound matters.

Notes

1 Oscar Wilde as quoted in Susan Sontag, *Against Interpretation* (London: Vintage, 1994), p. 3.
2 For a more detailed analysis of this bias in established film scholarship see Chapter 3.
3 Interestingly, the period I am investigating has been dubbed by some as 'the second coming of sound'; see Charles Schreger, 'The Second Coming of Sound', *Film Comment* (Vol. 14, Issue 5, 1978), pp. 34–37.
4 The increasing reliability of digital technologies means that, for example, Spielberg could supervise the final mix of *Jurassic Park* – done at Lucas's Skywalker Sound near San Francisco – whilst in Poland directing *Schindler's List*. Digital tie-in lines allowed full quality sound to be played back in real time to Spielberg across the ocean.
5 Rick Altman, 'The Material Heterogeneity of Recorded Sound', in R. Altman (ed.), *Sound Theory, Sound Practice* (New York and London: Routledge, 1992), p. 16.
6 Virtually all of the interviews that I carried out for this book were either preceded or followed by some 'unscripted' social interaction, be it a meal or a more informal chat.
7 One example: Larry Blake was the supervising sound editor for Steven Soderbergh's Oscar-winning *Traffic*. Blake supervised also the 2.0 mix for home release on video, a separate 5.1 mix for DVD, the M&E (music and effects) version for the foreign markets, the version for airlines, as well as travelling to the key European markets to supervise the quality of the dubbing in multiple foreign languages.
8 Tom Levin, 'The Acoustic Dimension: Notes on Cinema Sound', *Screen* (Vol. 25, Issue 3, May/June 1984), p. 63.

1

The Dolby phenomenon

> When it comes to film sound, no name is more familiar to audiences than Dolby. (Dolby Labs pamphlet)[1]

The term Dolby has been employed in academic writing mostly to refer to a set of technological innovations affecting mostly sound reproduction. It is tempting to follow this approach and study Dolby as a means to investigate said new technologies. However, I would like to suggest that Dolby's achievement goes considerably further than a technological shake-up. In the 1970s and early 1980s, Dolby achieved nothing less than a comprehensive industry-wide transformation, from studio attitudes to sound, filtering through to film-makers' creative use of sound and audience expectations. Dolby achieved this whilst creating one of the most successful companies in the history of the entertainment industry. Some figures might help give some measure of the size and success of Dolby Laboratories. With one exception, all post-1977 Oscar winners in the Sound categories have used Dolby-encoded soundtracks.[2] Dolby-licensed products have surpassed the staggering figure of over 1 billion products sold. There are nearly 70,000 Dolby-equipped cinema screens around the world and more than 12,000 films have sported a Dolby-encoded soundtrack since the early 1970s. Mixing facilities employing Dolby technology are currently available in 43 countries. Dolby Laboratories have been granted 616 patents in 28 countries, and 645 trademark registrations in 95 countries.[3] Figures like the ones above tell a story of success even to the uninitiated eye of such size and scope to support the need for investigating the Dolby phenomenon in ways that go beyond technological prowess. Most remarkably, Dolby Labs have managed to establish themselves as a market leader and have maintained their position over a period of more than 30 years, a feat never matched by any other company dealing with film sound.[4] How has Dolby achieved this and what are the implications of this achievement?

In order to understand the full magnitude and importance of the changes that Dolby has brought to the industry we need to take a few steps back and review the state of play before Dolby entered the frame. Warner Brothers introduced synchronous film sound in the late 1920s. This widely known and reported piece of cinema history has been written about mostly in relation to the changes that it ushered in, both in terms of its impact on filmmakers and, to a lesser extent, audiences. However, little has been said in relation to what actually did not happen. Indeed, one of the central assumptions common to most writing on the coming of sound has been that sound innovators succeeded spectacularly both in terms of the speed of adoption of sound on film by studios and in terms of the universal acceptance with which the talkies were received by audiences worldwide. Cecil Hepworth expresses this view in touchingly personal terms:

> To me the most remarkable thing about this union (of talking machines and cinematography) is the speed and completeness with which it has been accomplished. Until two or three years ago the high contracting parties were completely aloof from one another, and although from time to time there were rumours of an engagement, it was not until quite recently that the mating took place.[5]

However, the history of the coming of sound is as much a history of stunted development as it is one of unprecedented growth. As studios were eager to cash in on the novelty of sound (synchronised speech to be more precise) on film, they rapidly moved from a cautious approach to sound to an all-talkies policy within a few years from the release of *The Jazz Singer* in 1927.[6] Exhibitors worldwide also made sure they would join in on the new sound craze and take full advantage of the new financial horizons that had opened before them.[7] However, almost inevitably, the earlier systems had imperfections and limitations that quickly became obvious to the industry. Although the technology improved quickly, it soon became apparent that there was no desire on the part of exhibitors to replace the sound equipment they had just spent a considerable amount of time and money to install with the new technology, despite the potential improvements in quality. Clearly the relationship between quality and cost was deemed, perhaps understandably, less attractive than it was originally hoped for. This had a de facto limiting effect on both the early production and reproduction of film sound. In some important ways, sound on film had become too successful too quickly.

A telling example of this problem is the failed adoption of improved loudspeaker design developed by several manufacturers in the mid- and late 1930s. In particular, MGM had developed what became known as the Shearer Two-Way Horn System. This new loudspeaker was revolutionary in that it improved dramatically the reproduction of both high and low frequencies. This was perceived as a need by studios because the frequency range they were able to use during production had grown wider since the late 1920s and allowed them to be much more 'adventurous' with sound, as well as guaranteeing more faithful sound recordings. Remarkably for its time, this two-unit speaker could provide a 40–10,000 Hz uniform frequency response (the maximum spectrum audible to humans is 20–20,000 Hz). It also helped reduce amplifier background noise. Indeed, the Academy sanctioned the relevance of this innovation by awarding MGM a special Technical Award. It was not long before another manufacturer giant, Western Electric, developed a sound system that had the Shearer System at its core. The 'Mirrophonic' sound system was the next evolutionary step forward for sound reproduction in cinemas, and it was ready as early as 1938. However, despite the Shearer's remarkable success, when Western Electric attempted to market the new system they found that only a handful of exhibitors were willing to re-equip (it was not a matter of a simple upgrade: a new speaker system needed installing and even the projector would require some attention to accommodate the new system). The system never reached a significant number of cinemas.[8]

When, in the late 1930s, it finally became clear that there was no scope for the adoption of further technological improvements that involved substantial investment on the part of exhibitors, attention turned to the issue of standardisation. If new sound technology was not going to be adopted by exhibitors then the creation of a universal standard was, for the first time since the inception of sound on film, a distinctive possibility. The attraction of standardisation mainly resided in the need to ensure that all films produced would sound 'acceptable' in virtually any sound-equipped cinema in the

world. This was not an unusual enterprise: the pursuit of standardisation of one kind of another had been at the forefront of sound
makers since the eighteenth century, when Joseph Sauveur, a French
physicist, proposed that the note C should equal 256Hz. The drive
for standardisation became more acute when instruments for the
recording and transmission of sound over distance became more
common. In particular, the telephone is an excellent example of how
technology 'settled' for a standard that, whilst only covering a
minority of the sound spectrum, was deemed an acceptable standard
for the transmission of the voice.[9] This new-found desire for standardisation ought to be played against the increasing awareness that
another kind of standardisation, speechless movies, was now clearly
lost forever.[10] The idea of employing a worldwide common currency
as far as sound recording and reproduction was concerned was an
attractive proposition in the face of the (potential) loss of universal
appeal due to the introduction of speech, and thus different languages, in talkies. In 1938, the Academy of Motion Picture Arts and
Sciences began studying the possibility of adopting a standard theatre playback response curve (i.e. what films would sound like in an
average theatre). After some tests, an agreement was reached and the
'Academy Curve', which was to dominate for nearly fifty years the
understanding of what filmmakers could expect their audiences to
hear in cinemas, was born. The Academy characteristic, as it also
became known, prescribed a rather limited frequency response
(rolling-off high frequencies such that the response heard in the theatre is 20dB down at 10kHz), and, more damagingly for the quality
of sound reproduction, it showed little concern with regard to
theatre acoustics.[11] The Academy characteristic did indeed achieve
standardisation across the globe but at a high price. The developments in sound technology of the late 1930s, 1940s, 1950s, 1960s
and early 1970s were only marginally adopted. Although film sound
was still in its infancy, its growth was being stunted.

It would be difficult to overestimate the problems caused by this
early decision. The frequency range and quality of sound in most
cinemas was not much better than that of telephones and continued
to remain so until the mid-1970s, until, that is, the arrival of Dolby.[12]
There had been, as I mentioned earlier, several attempts at improving
sound reproduction, but the inconsistency in availability both of films
and properly equipped theatres meant that filmmakers could never
confidently employ anything other than monophonic sound, a limited

frequency range, and inadequate loudspeakers in cinemas whose architecture was still a reminder of the vaudeville days. As John Belton points out: 'The magnetic revolution proved to be more of an in-house shake-up than an industry-wide transformation'.[13] Cinema architecture also suffered and remained firmly rooted either in the Grand Picture Palace tradition or in the small local cinema variety.[14]

It is not possible to gauge fully the extent to which this early drowning of the infant actually affected the development of sound aesthetics, and coloured the work of film scholars. However, one indisputable fact remains: poor quality sound had been the industry standard worldwide for nearly forty years by the time Dolby Laboratories set out to rectify this. In short, Dolby's project was ambitious in ways that went beyond the simple technological dimension. What was at stake was less a matter of introducing new technologies and more a question of changing attitudes towards film sound amongst filmmakers, industry executives and, ultimately, and most importantly, exhibitors. Indeed, the awareness of this complex task was at the forefront of Dolby's thinking, as these words from a Dolby Labs pamphlet emphasise: 'Dolby's new film format required significant changes throughout the film sound recording/producing chain, and thus throughout the film industry.'[15]

The question here becomes: who is Ray Dolby and how has he achieved this change?

The man behind the wheel: Ray Dolby

Although I do not wish to fall into the 'trap' of the Great Man Theory, there is no doubt that the company at the centre of this study, Dolby Laboratories, owes much to his founder. Many collaborators have played a key role over the years as in the famous case of Ioan Allen, the British engineer responsible for most of the Dolby Stereo programme. Indeed, the term Dolby here mostly stands for the company rather than its creator, American engineer and physicist Ray Dolby. Raised in the area that was to become the hotbed of film sound, that is, the West Coast of America (he was born in Portland, Oregon but his family soon moved to San Francisco), Dolby joined multimedia giant Ampex when he was only fifteen. His time at Ampex was significant because it provided him with an opportunity to work for a leading company involved in the development of new audio and video technologies. In particular, Ampex developed in

1954 the first magnetic theatre sound system, manufactured for
Todd-AO and Cinemascope. Ampex manufactured the magnetic
strip that the 4-track (Cinemascope) and 6-track sound channels
(Todd-AO) were recorded on before being married to the 70 mm
filmstrip. Ray Dolby (who eventually joined the team that produced
in 1956 the first 'practical' videotape recorder, the Ampex VRX1000
or Mark IV) was clearly in the right place to learn about magnetic
sound recording and the two famous problems that plagued it: the
cost of prints and reproductive equipment (magnetic sound prints
could cost up to ten times that of conventional mono optical prints),
and the limited life of the magnetic tracks (which deteriorated far
more quickly than in the case of optical mono prints because of the
friction with the 'reading' head). In this sense it is important to note
that 3M, the company responsible for the development of the first
production line of magnetic tape for sound recordings, was also
behind Ampex's attempt at recording video as well as audio on magnetic tape. Bob Hern, an engineer with 3M, proposed as early as
1948 the idea of audio-visual recording on magnetic tape. Indeed,
3M manufactured the tape and Ampex provided the hardware for
the first ever demonstration that took place at the 31st annual convention of the National Association of Radio & Television Broad-
casters (NAB) on 15 April 1956 in Chicago. In short, Dolby had been
at the epicentre of a historical and technological development by two
leading companies in the field of sound recording. In light of these
early experiences, his decision to turn his attention to finding a solution to the problems of noise reduction and limited frequency range
when he created Dolby Laboratories in the mid-1960s is hardly surprising. The music industry was the first beneficiary of Dolby Labs'
noise reduction system. Background hiss and frequency range were,
once again, the obstacles and Dolby knew he had the answer to both.
In particular, Dolby Labs produced two noise reduction systems.
One, Dolby 'A', was destined for professional products only, the
other, Dolby 'B', for consumer products (see page 39 for further discussion of the technology involved and its implications). The success
of the Dolby noise reduction system was apparent almost immediately: since the first appearance of the Dolby 'B' noise reduction
system on a tape player built by Nakamigi in Japan the name Dolby
and noise reduction have become inseparable.[16]
    Ray Dolby had also shown a remarkable sense of timing in
investing in the music industry at a time of profound change. Dolby

Laboratories had seen the light of day in England (although the company was registered as an American interest) in 1965. That is to say, Ray Dolby's company was formed in the middle of one of the most revolutionary decades as far as sound recording, reproduction and consumption are concerned. During the post-war period, cinema sound had maintained a substantial lead in the field of sound reproduction with respect to other forms of entertainment. In the case of home record players, for example, the technology was still rather rudimentary: speakers had a very limited frequency range, as well as substantial background hiss. Although most cinemas were suffering from similar problems, by the mid-1950s it was possible for cinemagoers, especially those living in large cities, to experience stereophonic sound coupled with widescreen formats. Twentieth-Century Fox's insistence on producing 4-track magnetic sound-tracks for all its Cinemascope releases (a policy directly enforced by Fox's head Spyros Skouras) meant that a high-quality sound reproduction system was available to the general public, despite the relatively limited availability of both prints and cinemas able to reproduce stereophonic sound. Indeed, together with widescreen processes, the availability of stereophonic sound was a key 'weapon' in the war Hollywood was waging against the new threat that television posed.[17]

The introduction of new widescreen formats, such as Todd-AO and similar 70 mm systems (most of which employed 6-track magnetic stereo) meant that an increasing number of films were available to the public that could rely on good sound quality and stereophony (the meaning of the word 'stereo' will be discussed later). However, as it was in the case of their main predecessor, Cinerama, the cost of both prints and cinema installation drastically limited the overall impact on audiences and filmmakers, as we shall shortly see in detail. Thus, when Dolby entered the scene, cinema sound was showing clear signs of regress (the number of stereophonic films and stereo-equipped cinemas peaked in the mid-1950s and eroded quickly after that until a virtually complete regression to mono sound in the late 1960s and early 1970s).[18] At the same time, the music industry was enjoying a period of unprecedented change through the explosion of rock and roll music and the development of home hi-fi systems. In a reversal of what had been true in the 1950s and early 1960s, the quality of sound reproduction in the home now easily surpassed, in principle at least, the average movie theatre in terms of sound

quality as the latter was still stuck with desperately antiquated technology. Moreover, the popularity of large live rock concerts tipped
the balance of sound quality firmly in favour of forms of entertainment (and entertainment 'spaces') other than the cinema. It is therefore not surprising that many innovators working in or around the
field of sound recording and reproduction began to explore these
new possibilities. Indeed, Dolby was not the only one to have spotted the potential. Two giants of entertainment – Kodak and RCA –
were also working at the same time on a stereophonic sound system
for movies that would retain the quality of aforementioned magnetic
systems but at a substantially lower cost to both studios and
exhibitors. In this sense, Dolby was in an almost ideal position to
make the move from music to cinema sound. He had successfully
developed and implemented a solution to one of the longest-stand-
ing problems plaguing sound recording and reproduction. He had
knowledge of the music industry. He was an American who had
lived in England (where he completed a PhD in Physics at the University of Cambridge) and he had been exposed to some of the most
influential cultural movements that were shaping new generations of
consumers. In many ways, he was the proverbial man in the right
place at the right time.

Dolby Labs set out in the late 1960s to develop their 'Dolby A'
system for cinema application. Building on the 'Dolby A' professional system for the music industry, Dolby Labs began to develop a
similar system for movies. It would work on the same principle as
'Dolby A', namely to reduce background hiss, hence allowing soundtracks to extend their frequency range without incurring an exces-
sive amount of hiss and distortion. This was a particularly acute
problem in movies: although post-mixing technology had improved
substantially over the years, post-mixing of multiple tracks without
any major loss of quality still remained the exclusive domain of magnetic soundtracks. This was a time when movie theatres were stuck
in a time warp. They either continued to employ the same monophonic equipment that had been installed decades earlier, or were
unable to make use of their magnetic stereo equipment simply
because there were no magnetic stereo prints available any longer. In
this climate, the application of 'Dolby A' noise reduction to movies
was a logical step forward.[19]

The birth of an era: the origins of the Dolby Stereo system

As early as 1970 Dolby had proven that the 'Dolby A' noise reduction system could be successfully applied to movie optical soundtracks with excellent results. Dolby, like all technological innovators before him, knew that developing the right wares and proving that they work is only the first step. He now needed to lobby the film industry to convince them of the advantages of his new system. His strategy was clear: taking a leaf from his experience in the music industry, where 'Dolby B' encoded cassette retained an acceptable sound quality even when played back in non-Dolby players, Dolby and his collaborators, first among which was Ioan Allen, argued with the industry that only one Dolby-encoded print would be necessary for general release. In other words, the main aim was to quash fears that adopting the new system would mean having to produce two prints, one for Dolby-equipped theatres and one for those without, hence incurring in precisely the kind of additional costs that had ultimately wrecked previous sound innovations. Success for Dolby's film sound system proved to be more elusive than expected. The 'simple' improvement of sound quality on mono prints that Dolby had achieved impressed filmmakers and studio executives but did little in terms of convincing exhibitors that the improvement was worth the expense required to upgrade film theatres (as well as studio recording and mixing technology). In many ways, Dolby had hit the same brick wall that previous innovators had met since the coming of sound: modest, though technologically significant, improvements in sound technology could not shift industry-wide attitudes. Ironically, it was perhaps this initial failure (one that Dolby's literature refers to as 'a very slow start') that proved to be the catalyst for the revolutionary contribution that Dolby Labs were to make to the cinema industry. If studios, exhibitors and the general public were to be won over, it would be necessary to provide them with nothing less than the missing link in film sound, something that had eluded all of his predecessors: an economically viable, universally available optical stereophonic system married to conventional 35 mm prints. The time of Dolby Stereo had finally arrived, although the task was daunting, encompassing virtually all aspects of the industry, from cost to software availability, and from manufacturing to marketing.

Crucially, Dolby and his collaborators understood that in order to be successful his system would have to be compatible with existing

sound installations, and thus be relatively easy to install. This trans-
lated into cheaper installation than any other previous stereo sound
systems: the cost of Dolby conversions, less than $5,000, was, as
Michael Arick emphasises, 'easily within the reach of most first-run
houses'.[20] The financial feasibility of Dolby Stereo is particularly evident if one considers that the price tag for Cinemascope 4-track
magnetic sound in the 1950s was around $25,000, and that Disney's
Fantasound in the 1940s cost over $45,000 to install. Dolby's choice
was based on a choice of strategy informed more by market necessi-
ties than technological and aesthetic considerations. It is important
to note this because, in many ways, we have come to accept that the
meaning of the word stereo in the cinema is what Dolby Stereo (in
all its many incarnations) 'says' it is. Interestingly, the question of
what stereo should sound like had also been at the forefront of
debates when stereophonic sound was introduced in the 1950s.
During a presentation by John Hilliard, one of the key figures in the
development of cinema sound engineering, about Altec Lansing's
speakers and amplifiers for magnetic stereo reproduction in cinemas, a delegate from the Westrex Corporation (Dr JG Frayne) asked
the speaker: 'If he would like to define what is meant by true stereophonic sound.'[21] Mr Hilliard's reply testifies to the vagueness of the
term 'stereo' in the cinema: 'I do not have any simple answer to the
question. I think we will all have to struggle through this thing until
we finally find an ultimate position which gives good stereophonic
reproduction'.[22] However, he also stated in the same presentation
that it was Altec Lansing's view that widescreen processes required
'a minimum of three-channel stereo sound'.[23] Dolby Stereo is also
based on this principle, which I would like to call the 'one-wall' narrative principle. It follows an established loudspeaker placement
pattern, whereby images on screen have three sound sources/
channels behind the screen (left, right and centre) with a fourth
channel (surround) employing an array of speakers emanating non-
directional sound from around the auditorium.

   This design follows the principle that audiences should be offered
directional sound (i.e. sound whose direction could easily be identifiable) only from one wall of the auditorium, namely that where the
screen is placed. The notion at the core of this thinking is that sound
emanating from somewhere other than an onscreen source would
cause the audience to get distracted in an attempt to locate the origin
of that sound, hence disrupting the narrative flow. Thus, the implied

suggestion is that the surround channel be employed only in a diffuse, non-directional manner so as not to 'disturb' the narrative.[24] Despite implicitly suggesting that primary information ought to originate from the screen, the one-wall principle did away with the need to deal with complicated alternatives, like additional surround channels, that would have meant a serious rethink of the meaning of stereo in the cinema.[25]

Dolby was now in a position to go back to the industry with his truly remarkable breakthrough and hope for a better response than it had been in the case of Dolby System noise reduction. However, as this extract from Dolby's own literature clearly emphasises, once again technology was not going to be enough to win the day:

> Whereas Dolby noise reduction for professional tape recording was a relatively straightforward add-on and could be marketed as such, Dolby's new film format required significant changes throughout the film sound record/reproduce chain, and thus throughout the film industry. Dolby's ultimate goal seemed simple enough: to profit from the manufacture and sales of a new range of theatre sound-processing equipment. However, for that to happen, film producers had to be educated in the benefits of the new format. Sound mixers had to be brought on stream with new techniques. Distributors had to be reassured that stereo release prints were compatible with mono theatres. Theatre equipment suppliers had to be educated in system requirements and installation procedures. In addition, theatre owners had to be convinced that investing in the new equipment would pay off at the box office. As a result, it was necessary to implement and staff a film sound programme to reach out to all these disparate segments of the film industry.[26]

The winning formula: Dolby's licensing and marketing policy

Although the developments outlined above might help explain how Dolby identified what 'kind' of technology was most likely to succeed, it still does not explain entirely why he was so successful at it, and how Dolby Labs have managed to provide the most widely used cinema sound technologies since the 1970s. Perhaps the strongest clue in this sense is to be found in the company's approach to licensing and marketing.[27]

Dolby's licensing strategy is organised around some cardinal points from which the company has never deviated. Developed very early on, suggesting careful planning and acute business sense, Dolby's licensing programme would appear to revolve around three cardinal points: (1) relationship with manufacturers, (2) royalty structure, and (3) quality control.

Relationship with manufacturers

Dolby's early decision to manufacture exclusively professional products signalled the intention to establish a very active licensing relationship with existing manufacturers of consumer products. Although cautious at first (Dolby exclusively licensed the use of 'Dolby B' for open reel recorders to one company alone, KLH, between 1968 and 1970), Dolby quickly moved on to a more 'aggressive' stance establishing relationships with a variety of players, and the choice of not relying solely on the quality of their product proved to be an inspired choice. The cautionary tale of Sony's Betamax disaster, which saw Sony lose out to its competitors in the burgeoning VCR market because it stubbornly refused to license widely in the mistaken belief that technical quality only would win the day, further testifies to Dolby's savvy attitude. Most importantly, the policy adopted of not competing with licensees of Dolby technologies, unlike most other cases in the consumer electronics market, provided Dolby with an aura of commercial and intellectual independence.[28] Over the years, this feature has proven very useful in retaining its market leader position. Indeed, Dolby capitalises on this aspect in the company's publicity material when it emphasises that 'Dolby Laboratories is an independent company with no special ties to any particular film studio. Sound is our only business, as it has been for more than 30 years'.[29]

Royalty structure

If the kind of relationship with manufacturers that Dolby pursued was to withstand the test of time, it needed cementing with similarly 'friendly' financial arrangements. Dolby achieved this by introducing a royalty structure that has been kept at remarkably affordable levels over the years. This aspect of Dolby's licensing programme clearly aims at ensuring that manufacturers continue using Dolby technologies rather than looking elsewhere for cheaper alternatives. Once again, refusing to rely exclusively on the quality of his products, Dolby let the money do the talking. Licensing fees for most applications employing Dolby Digital or Pro Logic surround sound systems are around $10,000 and royalties are also considerably cheaper than one might otherwise expect, making it a little easier to understand how Dolby has been successful at maintaining its position at the top of the film sound ladder.

Quality control

However important financial and business considerations might be, Dolby's success has also been carefully protected by strict quality controls. These were created to ensure that quality standards were maintained in the face of proliferation of products incorporating Dolby technology manufactured across the globe by hundreds of different companies. This is a particularly important aspect, because Dolby's choice not to manufacture consumer products inevitably complicates the issue of quality control. Any manufacturer of software or hardware wishing to incorporate Dolby technology in their product needs to undergo a specific process of planning and testing. At any point during this process, Dolby laboratories have the right to stop the process on grounds of quality. Indeed, Dolby licences are only issued if these strict quality controls are met satisfactorily. It is important to note that such quality controls refer in equal measure to financial stability and technical ability.

What is the overall picture that comes out of these considerations? Unlike most accounts of the historical development of Dolby Laboratories, it is possible to identify Ray Dolby's intention to go into the cinema market as pre-dating his interest in the music industry (see interviews with Ioan Allen and Ray Dolby on pages 36 and 91). The drive to establish Dolby as a player in the cinema market inevitably helped to shape the kind of technology Dolby Labs would develop as well as the kind of market dynamics they would have to deal with. Dolby's financial and marketing strategy was achieved through the creation of a continuing relationship with customers rather than in a one-off purchase of Dolby products and licences. The relatively modest royalty rate still found today remains the most obvious example of this strategy.

Awaiting a champion: the need for 'the right film'

By the mid-1970s everything was in place, from technology to manufacturing, to ensure Dolby's success. However, despite having

solved all technological obstacles and having overcome initial resis
tance on the part of exhibitors, the rate of adoption of the Dolby
Stereo system remained frustratingly slow. Only a handful of theatres worldwide had converted to the new system. The problem was
a common one to new technological standards: in order for the
hardware to be successful, it is crucial to have the software that can
be played on it. Although there had been a few titles released in
Dolby Stereo, such as *Tommy*, and *A Star is Born*, Dolby was still in
search of the perfect vehicle for his wares. Logically perhaps, studios
had shown an interest in Dolby's technology as a way to enhance the
impact of musicals. This policy echoed the situation of the 1920s,
when it was musicals such as *Don Juan* and *The Jazz Singer* that had
first sported sound technology. However, generic aural conventions
of musicals, with their emphasis on front channels for the majority
of aural material and their use of rear channels mostly for music
only, limited severely the overall impression that surround sound
could have on audiences. In many ways, the sound dynamics of
musicals were too similar to those of the records that audiences
could play in their homes. In short, Dolby needed a 'special' kind of
movie: a champion for its wares, which differed substantially from
the kind of movies that had used its technology until then. More
importantly perhaps, Dolby needed a new kind of filmmaker –
someone who understood technology and its potential and was not
afraid of using it. The time was ripe for one of the most momentous
cooperations in the history of cinema. And despite the interest and
help that studios such as Pinewood and Elstree had shown in the UK,
the 'missing link' was to come from the other side of the ocean.

A match made in heaven: *Star Wars* and Dolby

By the mid-1970s, it became legitimate to wonder whether the
creative opportunities that Dolby's developments had engendered
would be matched by a change of similar magnitude in aesthetic
terms. George Lucas's 1977 Twentieth-Century Fox space epic
Star Wars was the film that, more than any other, answered Dolby's
'challenge'. The film's soundtrack went further into exploring the
potential of the newly available technology than any other film
that had preceded it. Crucially in terms of the development of the
Dolby era, the film represented the most successful example of the
collaboration between a new generation of sound technicians and

sound-conscious directors whose formation was deeply rooted in the 1960s rock (and aural) revolution. Indeed, Lucas has often emphasised the fact that the average age of filmmakers involved in the production of *Star Wars* was mid-twenties. The result of that collaboration was nothing less than a breakthrough in both sound production and exhibition. From sound architecture to spatial awareness, from sound texture to detail, from mixing to editing, from voice characterisation to physical sound, the film introduced a concept of sound that was finally willing to abandon its traditional shyness and move forward to claim a primary role.

Although the success of *Star Wars* is not directly imputable to one single element, a combination of economic and institutional factors can help us understand why it can be regarded as the real turning point in the history of contemporary sound, hence the Dolby era. The technological developments I described earlier took place at a time when filmmaking practices were undergoing significant changes in Hollywood. Lucas himself was in the mould of a new emerging figure of filmmaker – one that, though floating adrift of Hollywood in a geographical and political sense, still kept those shores firmly in sight. As Steve Neale has observed, this somewhat paradoxical figure was in fact 'dedicated to the aesthetics and values of the studio based, classical Hollywood movie, dedicated to narrative, action, spectacle, identification and genre'.[30] The aim of the so-called movie brats generation of filmmakers was not to replace existing Hollywood production patterns but to explore their boundaries, often in the light of recent technological developments. Sound was one of those boundaries. In the case at hand, Lucas and, perhaps even more crucially, his producer Gary Kurtz demonstrated this new attitude by approaching film sound not at a post-production stage, as was customary (and to a certain extent continues to be today), but as an integral part of the creative process from the very beginning.

A key decision in this sense was to begin discussions on the way the film would approach sound in the pre-production stages of the film, as early as 1975. This move, a rare occurrence in Hollywood then as it is now, signalled the filmmakers' intention to consider sound both in terms of production and exhibition, the latter in particular remaining the weak link in the sound chain. Dolby quickly realised the potential that the specific film genre, science fiction, offered, especially in view of the fact that previous efforts had

mainly concentrated on musicals. As vice-president of Dolby Laboratories (and one of the key figures in the development of the Dolby
Stereo programme), Ioan Allen comments: 'From Dolby's point of
view the subject matter would allow them to show their wares in a
way more demonstrative than was common'.[31] This 'synergy'
allowed Lucas to employ confidently both 35 mm and 70 mm prints
because the new technology would be available in both formats (70
mm prints were to employ a new type of encoding designed to
emphasise sub-bass response). Dolby engineers also visited the
sets of *Star Wars* before shooting began, in an attempt to optimise
results in the production stage (once again, both of these decisions
were unprecedented). Kurtz and Lucas understood that, despite the
importance of the technical and organisational relationship with
Dolby's team, *Star Wars* needed not just a new sound system, but a
whole new 'world' of sound. In an inspired and crucial move for the
development of today's sound aesthetics, Lucas hired Ben Burtt,
the man who was to become the key figure in the creation of the
new sound universe that both Dolby and Lucas hoped for and relied
on for the success of the movie. As Burtt himself remembers: 'They
[Lucas and Kurtz] just gave me a Nagra recorder and I worked out
of my apartment near USC for a year, just going out and collecting
sound that might be useful.'[32] Because of the unprecedented amount
of time Burtt was allowed in 'designing' the sound for the movie (he
is perhaps the first sound maker to have been allowed that level of
independence and freedom) Burtt created a new range of recorded
sounds rather than simply employing existing sound libraries, something that played a vital role in the success of the movie.[33] Finally,
and perhaps most importantly, the key factor in the relationship
between Lucas and Dolby was a certain degree of confidence that
here was a unique opportunity to change sound exhibition radically.
There is evidence of this in some of the choices made concerning
both production and distribution. In the former case, all stages of
sound recording (including foley, effects, dailies and ADR) were
Dolby encoded, and sound recordists were asked not to boost
high frequencies (a practice usually employed to improve dialogue
intelligibility but at the expense of dynamic range) – this was to
improve distortion levels during play back in Dolby-equipped theatres that employed wider dynamic ranges than standard theatres.
As for distribution, *Star Wars* was to be released in the Dolby Stereo
format, in both 35 mm and 70 mm prints, in over 50 per cent of

theatres during its first release wave. That is to say, Lucas intended audiences to hear what had been so carefully planned and orchestrated during production so that 'For the first time ever, the sound heard in the theatre should to all intents be identical to that heard by the director during the mix.'[34] These innovative practices and attitudes were light years from the classic Hollywood approach to sound. As Neale has pointed out, speaking of *Raiders of the Lost Ark*, for which Ben Burtt won another Academy Award: 'It uses an idea (the signs) of classical Hollywood in order to promote, integrate and display modern effects, techniques and production values in order to attract a modern audience'.[35] In this sense, Lucas's break with studio practices, though only partial, is significant, particularly because it had a positive effect in creating fertile ground for other filmmakers to depart from institutionalised practices when creating soundtracks, especially by employing new technologies.[36]

Hollywood as an industry was also being reshaped. New technologies apart from sound – such as cable television, satellites, pay TV, and videos – had provided Hollywood and other major entertainment industries with the possibility of forming new alliances, thus opening up new avenues for revenue. In sound terms, *Star Wars* contributed to the change mainly by boosting the diffusion of the Dolby Sound system. Interestingly, the opinions within Dolby as to the actual impact that *Star Wars* had on the awareness and sales of their sound system vary. Whilst there is general agreement that the success of *Star Wars* dramatically increased people's awareness of the existence of the Dolby Stereo system, some are more cautious as to whether the film had the same dramatic impact on sales. Ray Dolby himself (see interview on p. 36) suggests that sales data indicate a steady curve rather than one that dramatically peaks with *Star Wars*. Irrespective of whether *Star Wars* merely 'sped up' the adoption of Dolby's new system or substantially raised awareness, one thing remains obvious: Dolby's sales, already significant in the music industry, where its noise reduction system was rapidly becoming a standard, were to skyrocket to the point where Dolby Stereo became a standard in the film industry. The increase in film production costs represented a further important change at this time.[37] These were significantly on the rise (the average cost increased from $2 million to $10 million during the 1970s), thus delineating a clear need to maximise profit and attract new audiences. Most crucial, in this sense, was the realisation by Lucas and Kurtz that the possibility of

breaking with the low-fidelity monophonic sound tracks that had
become the industry's standard during the late 1960s and early
1970s could have an impact not only on production techniques but
also on audiences. The affordable Dolby stereophonic system, available to the vast majority of theatres through a relatively simple and
economical installation, resuscitated the meaning of the word
'stereo' for cinema audiences by dissociating it from very expensive,
road show 70 mm prints, mostly affordable only by large film theatres in major city centres. Dolby and Lucas were now in a position
to target effectively the hi-fi generation emerging from the late
1960s and early 1970s, and to bank on and consolidate Hollywood's young, under-30 audience that had replaced the formerly
dominant family audience.

Dolby consolidates and expands

The huge box-office success of *Close Encounters of the Third Kind*
immediately followed that of *Star Wars* in 1977. In this way, by the
late 1970s the name Dolby became associated not just with good
sound, but also with huge popular appeal, and an increasingly larger
number of filmmakers and studios adopted the new system. In particular, Dolby's visibility was greatly aided by the decision of adver-
tising the now famous 'double-D' logo on film posters worldwide
with the words 'In Selected Theaters' emphasising the presence of
Dolby as a mark of distinction.[38] More importantly, filmmakers
were beginning to single out sound as an element of distinction.
Steven Spielberg, the director of *Close Encounters of the Third Kind*,
remarked after the release of the film that 'It is of paramount importance to realise the acoustic dimension of movies. To experience
Close Encounters of the Third Kind in 70 mm 6-track stereo is
totally different from seeing it in mono'.[39] In this sense, Dolby's
contribution to the development of new sound aesthetics went
beyond simple technological prowess. The creation of the figure of
the 'Dolby consultant', one of the many new figures that have characterised the Dolby era was intended as a step towards ensuring that
filmmakers understood the technology and how to use it. However,
since Dolby consultants witnessed first-hand the development of
the new aesthetics of sound that the technology they supported had
made possible, they became a sort of 'conduit' for ideas amongst
different filmmakers. As Ioan Allen, one of the fathers of the Dolby

Stereo programme, emphasises, 'We were able to bring from movie A to movie B some new tricks and techniques they (sound people) had not thought of before'.[40] In other words, the advantage of employing Dolby technology for filmmakers did not stop at the level of wares: the exchange of ideas and practice amongst filmmakers highlighted the blurring of the traditional distinction between technicians and artists, at least as far as sound people were concerned.

The result of this exposure was an immediate increase in the number of exhibitors willing to upgrade their theatres to Dolby standards. *Star Wars* opened in 46 Dolby-equipped theatres in the USA. Only two years later, *Superman* opened in over 200 theatres with Dolby Stereo sound, and by 1981 over 2,000 theatres in the US were equipped with the new technology. When the Academy finally adopted Dolby's 'X-curve' as a standard for sound reproduction in cinemas to replace the old 'Academy Curve', it became clear that Dolby was no passing craze.[41]

Safe in the knowledge that a foothold had been firmly established, Dolby Labs went back to the drawing board. Despite the evident success of Dolby Stereo, filmmakers were demanding greater dynamic range in order to explore fully the potential that Dolby had unlocked. Dolby Labs had already tested a new system, Dolby SR, which had been developed for the music industry. Once again, the move was to apply this tried and tested technology to movies. In the summer of 1987 two films, *Innerspace* and *Robocop*, employed the new system. The improvement was drastic (increasing performance especially in terms of dynamic range), but despite initial success Dolby soon faced renewed demands by filmmakers for greater range and flexibility. The first wailing of digital technology had grown loud enough by this stage to be heard. In particular, Kodak had worked on a new system, CDS (Cinema Digital Sound), to provide digital sound capability to conventional 35 mm prints, and *Dick Tracy* and *Terminator 2* were amongst the first films to use CDS and thus optical digital sound. In so doing, Kodak had wrong-footed all competitors, including Dolby, but at a price. The digital track on Kodak's CDS replaced the analogue track, making digital prints incompatible with conventional analogue projectors and sound systems. Unsurprisingly, this choice effectively killed off CDS, but not before the potential that digital sound offered had been sampled. Indeed, by this stage of the Dolby era sound had become a lucrative

business and several companies and studios had joined the race for
digital sound. By the early 1990s, Dolby and two major studio-
owning companies, Sony and Matshushita, were developing their
own digital sound systems.[42] The Dolby era had entered the
digital stage.

Digital sound in the Dolby era

The arrival of digital sound in the early 1990s was significant both
in creative and institutional terms and ushered in the present stage
of the Dolby era. Three systems – Dolby Digital, DTS (Digital Theater Sound) and SDDS (Sony Dynamic Digital Sound) –appeared
almost simultaneously on the scene.[43] Dolby Digital premiered in
1992 with *Batman Returns*; the following year Sony introduced
SDDS with *Last Action Hero*, and MCA introduced DTS with *Jurassic Park*. In technological terms, there are substantial differences
between the three systems. Dolby opted for an optical system that
provides six discrete channels of sound: three front channels, two
rear surround channels and one 'extra' channel for subwoofer frequencies. This configuration is also commonly known as a 5.1
system. MCA/Matshushita chose a similar channel distribution
$(3+2+1)$ but opted for a sound-on-disc format whereby the soundtrack is delivered by means of two CDs played back by a special
reader that is kept in synch with the projector through an optical
track on the filmstrip. Sony's SDDS represents perhaps the greatest
departure from convention in that it provides, in its full version,
eight discrete channels of sound. In its full configuration $(5+2+1)$ it
resembles closely the golden era of magnetic sound with Cinerama
and Todd-AO whilst retaining the ease of distribution and flexibility
typical of an optical system. However, current mixing practices,
whereby films are made available in all three formats to avoid compatibility problems, has virtually killed off the 8-channel version of
SDDS, which is now used much more frequently in its scaled-down
6-channel version (employing the traditional $3+2+1$ configuration). Crucially, unlike CDS, all systems have a fail-safe mechanism
whereby conventional optical analogue ensures continuity should
the digital system fail, in order to avoid any disruption in the
presentation.[44] However, despite these technical differences, in
creative terms the three systems offer similar options. Indeed, the
$3+2+1$ configuration has now virtually become a standard for

digital presentation, just as it had been the case for optical analogue with the introduction of Dolby Stereo in the 1970s. Put crudely, the advantages for filmmakers are comparable to those the music industry enjoyed with the introduction of digital recording/mixing and the CD: increased dynamic range, virtually no hiss, faultless copies of original, improved frequency response and stereophonic surround (the latter had been, until the advent of digital sound, the exclusive realm of 70 mm 6-track magnetic sound only). The consequences for audiences are unquestionable, particularly in terms of exhibition. As we have seen, when *Star Wars* was first released in 1977 it was available in two different versions: a 35 mm, 4-channel optical copy and a 70 mm, 6-track magnetic copy. The latter, as we have seen, was largely available only to a few first-run theatres located in big cities. Consequently, only a comparatively small number of people had access to the subtleties of sound that had gone into the making of the film's sound track, despite the improvements that the Dolby Stereo system had brought in. Today, the availability of a single 35 mm, 6-channel digital copy in any one of the three main digital formats (Dolby Digital, DTS and SDDS) allows most spectators around the world to access the same sound quality that was once restricted to the few lucky ones who had access to 70 mm presentations.[45] Studios quickly began moving to an all-digital policy, and by 1995 Fox, Paramount and Warner had adopted an all-digital release policy.

What appears evident is that all major competitors in the race to digital have chosen to adhere to existing notions of what 'cinema stereo' ought to be. Both the configuration of speakers and channels, and the way film sound information is communicated to audiences have not changed, and the 'one-wall narrative' principle continues to be applied by most filmmakers and underwritten by technology. There are, however, signs that we might be about to enter a new stage of the Dolby era. That the new *Star Wars* trilogy should introduce, yet again, the latest development by Dolby Labs, Dolby EX, is confirmation of the fundamental role that these two companies have had in shaping the Dolby era. This particular development specifically originated from the demands of sound people. Lucasfilm's Gary Rydstrom, one the world's leading sound designers, suggested the new development as a response to a frustration he had perceived in terms of creative possibilities. More specifically, Rydstrom argued that present systems did not allow enough flexibility to filmmakers who might want to make greater, and more innovative, use of surround. To this effect, Lucasfilm and Dolby Laboratories designed an improvement to the existing Dolby Digital that now allows a new configuration, known as 6.1, whereby there is an equal number of three front and three rear channels. It is too early to assess whether we are on the eve of a reassessment of the relationship between screen sound and surround sound, but the indications are that this might be the case, especially in light of other developments that are still at the design stage. In particular, the move towards the digitalisation of movies has spurred some to design new systems that might deliver an increased number of channels, this time making use of 'top channels' (i.e. speakers mounted on cinema ceilings) as well as front and rear.[46]

Notes

1 Extract from *Why Should You Install Dolby Digital* pamphlet produced by Dolby Laboratories.
2 The exception is *Apollo 13*, winner of the Best Sound Academy Award in 1995.
3 Data available from Dolby's official web site at www.dolby.com (accessed 30 August 2003).
4 Despite this success, Dolby has remained a relatively small company with 550 employees worldwide and with annual revenues of around $120 million.
5 Cecil Hepworth, 'Preface', in John Scotland, *The Talkies* (London, 1930).
6 All films are US productions, unless otherwise stated.
7 For a fuller account of the coming of sound see Douglas Gomery, 'The Coming of Sound: Technological Change in the American Film Industry', in John Belton, and Elisabeth Weis (eds.), *Film Sound: Theory and Practice* (New York: Columbia University Press, 1985), pp. 5–24.
8 This should not detract from the undisputable success of the Shearer two-horn system that became a blueprint for future generations of speakers.
9 Interestingly, it is only at the beginning of the new millennium that telephone technology is finally being developed to handle wider frequencies, especially in the field of mobile telephony.
10 The rather peculiar experiment of the multi-language talkies, whereby the same script was filmed in three or more languages using the same sets and props but different actors, was, unsurprisingly, short-lived.
11 See Appendix 2 – Academy Curve and X-curve Comparison.

12   A new standard frequency response curve was eventually approved as a direct consequence of the introduction of Dolby technologies, the ISO 2969, also known as the 'X-curve'. For more information, see the ISO web site at www.iso.org (accessed 30 September 2002).

13   John Belton, '1950s Magnetic Sound: The Frozen Revolution', in Altman (ed.) 1992, p. 155.

14   Paradoxically, it was the supremacy of mono in the late 1960s and early 1970s that finally killed off so many of the old, large (1,000+ seats) auditoria and paved the way for new, more sound-friendly cinemas.

15   From *A History of Dolby Laboratories* – 11. The Dolby film programme available at http://dolbysearch.dolby.com/Company/is.ot.0009.History.html (accessed 30 August 2002).

16   The player Nakamigi built became available under the guise of three manufacturers: Advent, Fisher and Harman-Kerdan, who still continue the relationship with Dolby by manufacturing home cinema products featuring Dolby Surround technology.

17   As was the case with the rise of multiplex cinemas, it is interesting to note that this detail has regularly been overlooked in accounts of the 1950s Television vs. Cinema 'war'. Widescreen processes have traditionally been discussed almost exclusively in terms of screen size.

18   The best resource for investigating historical and technological issues concerning all widescreen formats is the American Widescreen Museum, available atwww.widescreenmuseum.com (accessed 30 August 2003). The site has also a rather comprehensive area dedicated to the sound systems employed in the various formats.

19   For more information on the development of Dolby technologies see my interviews with Ray Dolby and Ioan Allen later in this book.

20   Michael Arick, 'In Stereo! The Sound of Money', *Sight & Sound* (Vol. 57, winter 1987–88), p. 39.

21   John K. Hilliard, Conference presentation to the SMPTE (Los Angeles, 1 May 1953) – available at www.widescreenmuseum.com/widescreen/53stereo.htm (accessed 1 November 2003).

22   *Ibid.*

23   *Ibid.*

24   Indeed, when Lucasfilm originally detailed its recommendations for speakers to be approved under the THX system programme it specified that surround speakers ought to be dipole, i.e. emanating sound in a non-directional manner to emphasise a generic sound field rather than a directional one.

25   The one-wall principle is less a direct result of Dolby's chosen design and more of a continuation of a tradition in film sound. Even today most sound men and women adhere to the same guiding principle.

26 From A History of Dolby Laboratories – 11. The Dolby film programme available at: www.dolby.com/company/is.ot.0009.History.html (accessed 30 August 2002).

27 See also Dolby Laboratories Licensing Information available at www.dolby.com/trademark/co.ot.0204.LicInfo.pdf (accessed 1 September 2002).

28 The VCR is, again, a good example. Matshushita and JVC licensed VHS technology to several other manufacturers, but continued to manufacture VHS video recorders themselves.

29 Dolby publicity material.

30 Steve Neale, 'Hollywood Corner', *Framework* (Issue 19, 1982), p. 37.

31 Ioan Allen, 'The Dolby Sound System for Recording *Star Wars*', *American Cinematographer* (Vol. 58, Issue 6, July 1977), p. 748.

32 Mark Mancini, 'Sound Thinking', *Film Comment* (Issue 19, 1983), p. 45.

33 As a result, he was awarded an Academy Award for Special Achievements in Sound.

34 Mancini 1983, p. 45.

35 Neale 1982, p. 38.

36 This 'pioneering' role has been further qualified during the years by decisions he has made, such as to base his operations outside Hollywood (in San Rafael, near San Francisco), to create what has arguably become the most important sound facility in the world, Skywalker Ranch, and to initiate the THX and TAP programmes.

37 For a more in-depth analysis of the rise of a 'new', contemporary Hollywood see Jim Hillier, *The New Hollywood* (London: Studio Vista, 1992).

38 I asked Ray Dolby where the idea for the double-D logo came from. He explained that the first D stands for Dolby, the second, reversed D represents its perfect mirrored image. This signifies that with Dolby Systems every copy is exactly the same as the original recording.

39 Franco La Polla, 'Steven Spielberg', *Il Castoro Cinema* (Issue 99, May/June 1982), p. 8. My translation.

40 Extract from Christopher Cook, *Dancing Shadows*, a BBC – Radio 4 production (2000), part 3 of 4.

41 This new standard, codified as ISO 2969, is called X-curve (X stands for 'Extra') to distinguish it from the Academy Curve (also known as 'Normal Curve'). For more information, see the ISO official web site at www.iso.org (accessed 30 September 2002).

42 At the time, Sony owned Columbia Pictures and Matsushita owned MCA.

43 For more information see www.dolby.com (Dolby Digital), www.dtsonline.com (DTS), and www.sdds.com (SDDS) (accessed 30 August 2003).

44 The difference between the two can obviously be heard, and felt, by audiences, especially in terms of frequency and dynamic range, but it is understandably deemed to be of less inconvenience to audiences than having to stop and restart the film.

45 This mirrors Lucasfilm's overall preoccupation with standards of theatrical presentation as exemplified by his THX sound system and TAP (Theater Alignment Program) evaluation.

46 Dolby has recently tested a 'Top' channel for *We Were Soldiers* (2002). For more information see www.dolby.com/press/mp_pr_0209 _Soundelux.html (accessed 1 September 2003).

2

Interviews with the creators of Dolby: Ray Dolby

This is the first of two interviews – one with Ray Dolby and the other, later in this book, with Ioan Allen – aimed at providing a more detailed account of both how things happened and what impact they had on filmmakers and filmmaking. My intention, with both interviews, is to avoid a straightforward 'what happened when' and 'who did what' structure, much as that is to some extent inevitable. I hope to allow the personality of the two people who can easily be regarded as the two central figures to the development of Dolby Labs and its success to come to the fore. Their willingness to speak about doubts and failures as much as of success and conviction is significant in depicting not just the history of Dolby but also that of a particularly important period in the history of cinema, namely the late 1960s and 1970s. I have tried, much as I have done with the other interviews in this book, to preserve the dynamics of the interview as much as possible, limiting my editorial work to changes aimed at avoiding repetition.

The two interviews are particularly valuable because of their different emphasis. The interview with Ray Dolby traces the origins of Dolby Labs and the main thrust behind the company. That the company Ray Dolby formed should bear his name is no accident: reading his account reveals a life-long interest in sound and cinema that goes beyond business interest. Indeed, the 'human' element is perhaps one of the most interesting aspects of both interviews.

Ioan Allen also speaks often about individual directors and other filmmakers, and of the relevance of personal interaction. In an industry that it is often depicted as heartless and manipulative it makes for a refreshingly humanising effect.

The more exquisitely technical and biographical details form the core of the interview with Ray Dolby, whereas the interaction with the industry and filmmakers provide the backbone to the interview with Ioan Allen. In this sense the most important reason for allowing the interviews to appear in this format is because both Allen and Dolby's accounts elucidate the topic I am dealing with more directly and effectively than I could have anticipated.

Ray Dolby is a legendary figure. Indeed, he is so legendary that many people do not even know that he actually exists. The name Dolby has become so pervasive in our everyday life in some form or other that it is easy to forget that there is a man behind it. Although Ray Dolby is himself quick in pointing out the role that others have played in the Dolby Era there is little doubt that the overarching imprint on Dolby Labs originates from its founder.

Gianluca Sergi: I'd like to start from the beginning. I know that you went to work at Ampex early on. You were quite young.

Ray Dolby: Yes. I was first hired by Alex Poniatoff when I was still in high school. I was 16 years old. I had come to know him some months earlier, maybe in March of 1949.[1] He came to my high school and wanted to find someone who could run a film for his Mental Health Society film presentation. I was on the projection crew and I offered myself. I appeared and ran the projector for them. Afterwards he invited me to visit his company that had created the Model 200 professional audio tape recorder. He was very proud of his machine and wanted to show it to me so after the Mental Health film presentation we went to his [Ampex] plant in San Carlos [CA] and he gave me a demonstration. I was thrilled by this and at the end of it all he said 'would you ever like to work for me?' I said yes and he said he would give me a call whenever a suitable project opened up ... I did various projects [for Ampex]. I did the production engineering for a film and audio recorder synchroniser, which Ampex thought would be a good thing to introduce into Hollywood so that they wouldn't have to use optical recording any more to do their post-production work. Ampex developed the first really practical synchroniser and I did the production preparation for that, planning all of that.

Sergi: How much of the work you did then influenced your decision to go into your line of work, in other words noise reduction?

Dolby: Of course in those days, when you wanted to make a master tape you'd use the full width of the ¼-inch tape, so you had this enormous tape area. Not only that, the tape was running at 30-inches per second, and later 15-inches per second, so a lot of tape got used which meant that you had quite a good signal-to-noise ratio. It was only when people started trying to squeeze more tracks on the tape and running the tape slower and slower that they really came up against noise problems. There was a very slight 'hiss' that one could perceive with the Model 200 recorder, but it wasn't very much actually.

Sergi: How did you decide to get into noise reduction?

Dolby: I had my first noise reduction thoughts when I was working on the video tape recorder.[2] I thought 'this is where a noise reduction system would really be useful'. I'd heard about attempts not at video noise reduction but at audio noise reduction. People had been dreaming about audio noise reduction since the 1930s but it had a very bad reputation because no one had succeeded in making an effective noise reduction system without introducing undesirable side effects into the signal. It was pretty much sort of forbidden territory for a responsible engineering speculation. You couldn't go there because there had been too many, I won't say charlatans, but people with high expectations and inadequate engineering who had tried to solve the problem and it just did not work out; so the understanding was that no proper and responsible audio engineer would even get near that subject. But I kept flicking that idea around in my head for several years thinking that if anybody could solve this problem it would be a very, very valuable thing to have. Because I saw that the tapes were getting smaller and smaller with narrower and narrower tracks; a noise reduction system would be fantastic for restoring the performance of these small tapes to what could be achieved before when you could record faster and you had the whole tape for the track. So I thought about this when I was in Cambridge, and I thought about it a lot when I was in India.[3] It was in India, while I was doing some calculations on the distortions to be expected from one of the older noise reduction systems, that I suddenly realised that everybody else had been working at this problem from the wrong end. They were trying to manipulate the high amplitude loud signals and change them in some way that would bring the quiet signals up from the background. I said to myself what we need is a straight-through channel for the loud signals because the loud signals can take care of themselves, they don't need any manipulation. Any time you try to manipulate the loud signals all you do is introduce distortions. So I hit on this idea of the 'dual path process' whereby the quiet signals are amplified substantially when the signal is very, very quiet, but then you subject the signal to a very strong limiting process in a multi-band arrangement so that the low-level signal is amplified, but so long as it stays low level. As soon as it starts to get loud you say 'hey, you don't need any help any more', this is a loud signal, and the psychoacoustics characteristic of the ear will take over and make the noise essentially inaudible, the masking effect. I studied this matter while I was in India but I didn't have any resources to carry it through. On my way back from India to the UK, I thought about this question a lot. [I thought about it] especially on a trip back to the Far East that I took with Dagmar, who became my wife eventually. We spent two months visiting various manufacturers that I was interested in. I knew I wanted to set up a company, you see, so I thought it'd be good to find out what's happening in Japan and of course I was blown away by what I found there. On my way back I stopped in India, where we went to close down our house and then we started our overland drive. I stopped in Kabul, Afghanistan and spent some days writing up these ideas, and sent them off to my patent attorney in California, the same one who I'd used in connection with the video tape recorder. It was a two-month trip to get back to the UK; I proceeded to London and decided to go for it.

I went to the Decca record company. While I was in Cambridge I had done some recording projects of students' musical activities, and usually the students wanted to have the stuff transferred to disc as souvenirs. So I took my tapes down to the Decca studios in London and had them transferred, I had the pressings made. I got to know the people there, particularly Cyril Windebank and Bob Goodman.[4] I got back to London in May 1965: I went straight back to the Decca recording studios and I said to them 'I've got an idea for a way of reducing noise on master tapes. Would you be interested in that?' and they said 'if it works we would be VERY interested, because this is what we've been hoping for a long time, but there are actually a couple of systems sitting in our lab right now that have just come in for testing'.[5] That totally astonished me! I thought 'isn't this something!' What am I going to do? Am I going to hope that my idea is not similar to what these people are doing? But I decided to go ahead. I thought: what's the chance that after all this time they would have thought of the same concept that I had? So I decided to go ahead and design a noise reduction system. I took it back to them, and demonstrated it to them in November 1965 and they were delighted by what they heard. They put the most God-awful transient signal into it that they could devise, and piano music, guitar music and then finally orchestral recordings and they were very, very happy. They said 'we'd like to order some of these units'. The order did not come through until about March of 1966. I don't know why there was that delay, but I decided to plunge ahead and design a system and get it ready for production. It was a cliffhanger for me because I didn't know whether this order was going to come through or not. I checked with Bob Goodman or Cyril Windebank, who was the chief engineer, and he said 'I don't know what's wrong. It must be stuck in the bureaucracy somewhere'. Anyway, the order finally came through.

Sergi: And by this time the company was already formed. You had formed Dolby in 1965?

Dolby: Yes, May 1965.

Sergi: You were in the UK when you did this, but you created Dolby as an American company?

Dolby: No, I formed this, first of all, as a sole proprietorship and then my brother joined me and it became a partnership. Only after a couple of years, when I had to start thinking about getting some professional tax, international business advice and stuff like that, I went to Arthur Andersen. They were at the top of the list, that's why I selected them. I didn't have the time to do any research: I just knew they were one of the big apes at that time, and I thought that any one of them was going to be OK. One of the first things they said is 'look you are an American. There will be a lot of advantages in the long run for you if you establish the company as an American company, and you just have a UK branch', so that's what I did. Their reasoning related to future international sales, licensing and things like that. The UK was rather restrictive on a lot of these things and it was harder to do these things under UK law and taxation than under US conditions.

Sergi: You told me, before we started this conversation, that you always wanted to get in to movies.

Dolby: I was interested in high-fidelity sound, especially after I joined AMPEX in 1949. That was the highest fidelity sound that I'd heard up to that point. I knew what good sound could be and it absolutely amazed me that people were putting up with such bad sound in the movies. I mean the noise level was high, the noise level was modulated by the signal, it had a limited frequency response, and there was a lot of distortion, under both steady state and transient conditions, especially transient conditions. It was a mess! Somebody should do something about this, and as soon as I realised I had a noise reduction possibility, I thought 'this system is going to be useful for a lot of things'. I mean it can be used for master tape recording, it can be used for home tape recording, it can be used for reducing noise on disc recordings, and certainly on movie soundtracks. This system can make movie soundtracks sound better.

Sergi: Were you thinking specifically about optical soundtracks or magnetic as well?

Dolby: Both. As soon as I got my system up and running in 1966 and I delivered the first units to the Decca record company, I think I delivered about seventeen A3O1 units to them and then I realised I had to go out and find some other customers, and one thing that totally fascinated me was the possibility of the movie industry because I knew that that would require a lot of units. At that time using optical for the post-production process was past history; people were using mag [magnetic] film. So I went to the Elstree studios and met Tony Lumkin and Mike Bradbury and said 'I have got a noise reduction system here that will help you make better movies' and they were very interested in that, very receptive. This is part of a business, finding a lucky party who has been thinking about what you have been doing, the very thing you have been doing: 'Gee if we could just solve this problem, we'd have a much better product to offer and our customers would be happier'. They were beside themselves over the success of television, and especially colour television, because they saw that this was going to wipe movies off the map. Who's going to want to go to the movies any more if you can have a perfectly good high-quality presentation in colour in your own home? This was a big worry, and theatres were closing, movie attendance was falling off and so when I appeared and said I think I can help you make better movies they said 'we want you'. So it was wonderful [smiles]. That was about August 1966 and they made some test recordings using my noise reduction system on one of the post-production recorders and then transferring it to optical. The process reduced noise all right, but the quality was still very disappointing and I examined their equipment and found that their bias oscillators on their mag stripe recorders were operating at something like 40 kHz and you cannot make a high-quality recording using such a low bias frequency, you have to have 100 kHz at least, and I thought 'well, that's going to have to be tuned up' and then I find out that they were ... boosting their bass tremendously, which guaranteed distortion whenever you get a loud low-frequency sound, so that's on the post-production side. Then I realised that there was this problem with clipping and distortion and the heavy roll-offs used in the old Academy characteristic and the more I learned about it, the more questions I asked. I thought 'this is going to be a big project'.

This was going to be so different from the first thing I tackled, which was professional studio recording. With professional studio recording all the essential ingredients except one were in place. They had low wow and flutter, tape transport, you have a high bias frequency, you have a sensible equalisation on this being used, the frequency response is excellent. Just one thing and that is a high hiss level. So my noise reduction system was perfect for cleaning up the ills of professional studio recorders. Literally all you had to do was plug it in and just make sure your machine was reasonably lined up, but the combination of the two worked per- fectly together. I didn't have to go in and re-engineer the tape recorder and so it was easy for me to get the professional applica- tion of this noise reduction off the ground because of that good technical environment. So I could keep this new company in business by selling to this ready-to-go market and I looked at the movie project and I thought 'this whole thing is a can of worms; it's going to take me some time before I have a strong enough company to be able to do anything about this project'. So I let that lapse, but after about a year and a half or so, Tony Lumkin and Mike Bradbury came back to me and visited me in my lab on Wandsworth Road, and they said 'you've really got to do something here, we think you can do it, please work on this project!'. I said 'you know I'd love to but I just cannot afford it yet; just give me a little more time; you know these things are selling in the professional recording studio environment very well and I think in a year or so I can turn my attention to this, or two years'. So they went away disappointed but I kept watching this situation very carefully. As soon as I felt we had enough money, first of all I got us moved out of the tiny headquarters we were in and in to a larger space and then finally into a nice building on Clapham Road. I thought 'OK the money is coming in now, sales are good, now is the time to go after this movie project' and I thought 'well, maybe not quite yet let's just wait a little bit more'. In early 1969 I hired Ioan Allen and he seemed perfect as a marketing manager for our noise reduction equipment and he did a bang-up job selling these noise reduction units, especially the new units we had designed into the multi-track recording market. So in the 1969/70 period we were going gangbusters with the multi-channel recording scene. Eight-track, 16-track recording, 24-track recording hadn't really gotten started yet, and Ioan got practically all the major studios in London equipped with this stuff and then repeated the same thing in New York. So we began to have a firm base for bringing in enough money to do new projects, and that included licensing of the new B-type noise reduction system. That development was going on simultaneously, starting in 1967.

Sergi: That was the time of the compact cassette?

Dolby: The compact cassette had already been out and all it needed was some help in sorting out some of the same kinds of problems that the post-production and optical process had. Anyway, at a certain point I explained to Ioan my ideas about movie soundtracks, I said 'Go out there and really study this matter and figure out everything there is regarding the practices in the industry to find out why movie soundtracks are so bad'. I mean I knew some of the things, but I didn't know all of them, I wanted to get more information and get all the technical details. So Ioan went out and did that; he made a very thorough study of the matter and came back and said 'this is what we've got to do, that's what we have got to do'. Completely change the equalisation for example, get rid of the Academy curve: this is a revolutionary idea. Also tackle the ground noise reduction system, which had no anticipation in it so once the transient signal came along it just got clipped by the optical tape and that was it, a horrible distortion sound. Also increase the frequency response, study the falvanominators that were being used, see if we could raise the resonance frequency. Simultaneously there were all the issues in post-production recorders: increasing the bias frequency and regulating the bias so that if there were changes in line voltage and things like that you wouldn't have a different bias. A different bias by changing line voltage means you are going to get more or less distortion, wave form distortion and also a changed frequency response, or maybe more or less high-frequency distortion, intermodulation distortion. So Ioan and I went back to our old friends, Tony Lumkin at Elstree Studios, but Ioan also cast the net wider: he got to know the people at Pinewood and other studios and took trips to Hollywood to find out what their take on these things was. Our first noise reduction product was a very modest one. We couldn't count on being able to encode films right from the beginning, so we brought out a unit, Model 364 I think it was called, which was just a playback-only noise reduction unit with about 6 db of high-frequency noise reduction, and we sold a lot of those units.

Sergi: Who did you sell it to?

Dolby: Well, actually it was the Rank organisation that latched on to us: they had had a lot of success in selling anamorphic lenses, Cinemascope lenses. They had a kind of an exclusive on the Cinemascope lenses and they made a lot of money apparently selling these lenses all over the world and they saw our unit on the sound side as being a similar sort of gold mine. So they wanted to sign us up for this product for, I can't remember how long it was, maybe three years or something like that, and they were our exclusive agent for that time. They put this unit into all of their channels of distribution in all the countries that they were used to working in, which included not only Europe, but South Africa, Australia, New Zealand, etc.

Sergi: When Ioan Allen went to the industry with your product, what kind of response did you get from them? Were they interested?

Dolby: We never got such an enthusiastic response from anybody as we did from Tony Lumkin of Elstree Studios. I guess he must have been a very intuitive sort of guy; he thought about things: he realised that the movie industry was in danger of disappearing because people could hear better sound at home with their stereo sets. We are talking about the 1966/67/68 period. People had plenty good stereo systems then, and they were not used to listening to distortion, and yet when they went to the theatre, the cinema, that's what they got.

Sergi: OK so, when and how did you manage to convince people to start encoding films using your new noise reduction system?

Dolby: I think we made our own demo film. It was called *A Quiet Revolution* and it was done professionally. I mean we had professional movie crews coming in, sound crews and things like that, but we applied our noise reduction technology and ideas on how things should be improved to make the best possible soundtrack and we showed that demo film to a lot of people and then they got interested in the idea of trying it out for themselves on a short one-reel test, that sort of thing. It didn't happen overnight. These things happen more slowly than you might imagine because people have full schedules, they have got all kinds of projects that they are doing, and they don't want their boat rocked. Here's somebody coming in saying 'this is a great new idea do you want to try it out?' And they say 'oh my God, this is going to totally screw up my whole schedule for the new two months' or whatever, and so it takes time, they have to find the right time slot, to say 'OK, beginning of next month we will devote a couple of days to this project'. That's the way it went and of course you didn't know where you were going to have the success so you had to keep trying this studio, that studio, this person and that person, just hoping that you would get some traction somewhere.

Sergi: Was there anybody in particular that said 'yes, we want this'?

Dolby: Well, our first movie that was encoded was called *Callan*. It was a police sort of detective thriller. It was mono, but it had the first high-quality mono soundtrack. I think it was Elstree studios that did that. Ioan knows more about the details.

Sergi: I am actually going to speak to Ioan next month.[6]

Dolby: Yes, yes, that's good. He can give you much more detail than I can because he is the guy I started sending out to find out what was wrong and what we should do about it. He'd bring back the information and I and David Robinson would figure what we had to do with this in order to make products that would make sense.[7]

Sergi: From what I've read, either from Dolby's own literature or other sources, it seems that that first innovation, the introduction of noise reduction on mono optical tracks, played well with studios but exhibitors proved to be a bit reluctant.

Dolby: You know, the exhibitors would like to have a movie palace; they would like to have brand new carpets, air conditioning, and new screens and everything but they can't afford it. So very often when you approach a potential customer and he says 'I don't think I need this technology' what he is really saying is 'my budget is really hurting'. They'd like to lash out and spend a lot of money and have the best set-up imaginable. The movie business was really in bad shape; it seems much stronger today than it seemed in the 1960s. I mean there were articles appearing in newspapers about the end of movies and that sort of thing.

Sergi: The introduction of the first noise reduction system for optical sound tracks in Hollywood was obviously a big improvement. However, that's still nothing compared with the idea of going with stereo optical, which was a much bigger project in many ways. What made you think 'well, maybe now we should go and do something completely different'?

Dolby: Well, everything went step by step, I was very fortunate that Ron Uhlig of Kodak was very interested in the prospect of making stereo soundtracks on 16 mm film, and so we saw this as an opportunity to make stereo soundtracks on 35 mm film, just with a modified set-up, an optical set-up. Ron Uhlig agreed to engineer such a system for us and we brought it to the UK and used it for making the first stereo optical soundtracks. People were used to the idea of surround sound by that time, of course 70 mm films used surround sound and of course with 70 mm you had a pretty easy job of making fairly decent soundtracks: film was moving very fast, you could make wide tracks. The tracks on 35 mm 4-track were very narrow: it was very difficult to get good coating on the film. So since the fifties people were used to hearing surround sound once in a while at least, and it seemed natural to see whether we could at least produce stereo, and so that was the first attempt. We didn't jump straight to surround sound. Then we introduced a very crude dialogue enhancement circuit so that the dialogue could come out of the middle of the screen. It's a very bad thing if you have just two speakers, left and right: the dialogue would switch from one side to the other depending on where you're sitting in the auditorium, but we could artificially create a centre dialogue channel and that's what we did. But it wasn't very long before people movie producers said to us 'how about some surround sound?'

Sergi: They came to you?

Dolby: Well, it was sort of a combination. It's like the customers I was telling you about who are reluctant to do something because they cannot handle it right then. I felt that way about somebody asking me to produce a surround sound system. But of course we had just been through the whole quadraphonic era, which started in late 1969 and went through, I guess, about 1975 something like that. It came and went in the space of a few years, but during that time a lot of smart people had been cooking up various methods of getting four channels out of two channels and so we thought 'well, we might as well capitalise on that – maybe this is a legitimate application for this technology'. The whole quadraphonic thing flopped in the market place, but we thought maybe in the movie theatre it's a legitimate application and there's a need for it.

Sergi: I would be interested to know about the attitude that the industry had towards this [stereophonic optical sound].

Dolby: You know, I think it was a mixed thing. Some people were enthusiastic and some people said 'who needs more problems? My plate's full already!' and people like that are the ones who would say 'this guy who's enthusiastic about this doesn't know how this industry works, he doesn't know all the problems that we have'. So it's all very human stuff.

Sergi: Was it a conscious decision to make your system backward compatible so that it could be used with existing systems in film theatres?

Dolby: You mean whether we could use their loudspeakers, their amplifiers? Yes, we tried to do that wherever possible, but actually the theatres that were set up for multi-track and surround were very few and far between. It was only the few first-run houses around the country and that sort of thing. You had to be in places like Los Angeles or New York or London to hear these things, you couldn't hear them in Nottingham or Cambridge. It was new theatres and decent theatres that were still mono, but for one reason or another they sensed that here was an opportunity for upgrading and becoming newly competitive other than being drowned by television. That's where a lot of receptivity came from. People in the industry were really afraid of disappearing and they saw this as a life jacket thrown in their way.

Sergi: Let me ask you a little bit about marketing and licensing. What kind of strategies you chose at that point?

Dolby: Well, I can tell you that the film business side was a big money loser for many years, and I kept it going because I thought it just has to pay off eventually. People will appreciate good sound if we can get it into enough theatres, and there will be a pay-off.

Sergi: One of the things that was striking about your business model was the choice of not manufacturing consumer products.

Dolby: Yes. Well, that decision has several different aspects but I think the most important aspect is that the consumer market is a thousand times, ten thousand times bigger than the professional market in terms of the number of people you are dealing with. It's possible for one little factory to supply the world need for professional products, but the world need for consumer products of the same general kind is so great, orders of magnitude greater. When you go to a consumer electronics show, have you ever been to that? I mean it's just staggering how many people are making audio equipment and other consumer equipment and so it would be ridiculous of Dolby Labs to try to make its own brand of, let's say, cassette decks, because we would be in effect competing with our licensees. We can't license to all these licensees and then come out with the same product ourselves.

I knew this, and it was just amplified in my thought processes by Avery Fisher, of Fisher Radio, when I was negotiating the licence agreement, or explaining the licence agreement to him. He was quite concerned that there was nothing in there that said that I promised never to go into the consumer market and so he would like that put in, because he had had a bad experience. Hermon Hosmar Scott of Scott Radio in the late forties devised a noise reducer for use with phonograph records, it was a low pass filter with a sliding band and it sort of worked. Scott licensed that to Fisher and Fisher made these things and sold them on the consumer market, and then Scott decided to go into the business and sell them under his own name. This enraged Avery Fisher and he said 'this is what happened to me and I don't want this to happen again'.[8] So I explained to him that we couldn't even consider looking at the consumer market and it would be folly for us to go into competition with our licensees, so he didn't have to worry about that at all, because of the logic of it all. So that's why I don't think it's necessary to put anything into the agreement to that effect and he said 'well, I'll buy that'.

Sergi: You established licensing offices in the Far East early on.

Dolby: Well, I guess you could say that, in about 1971.

Sergi: Why did you do that?

Dolby: Because Japan was such a powerhouse of audio productivity that I had to make sure that I could take care of them. I had an office in New York by that time, I established that in 1968, and our second office was in Tokyo, but I did it by operating through a trading company. They were the official office, it's called Continental Far East. So obviously I provided all the technical information and told them what kinds of people to hire and things like that, and all the communications went through London. Licensees, you see, for the most part, don't read and write and speak English, and so we had to have somebody who could translate what we were doing to the licensees and answer their questions and come back to us with the problems. Hand-holding has been a key element in practically everything we have done, teaching people.

Sergi: One thing I wanted to ask you is about the 'image' of Dolby. It's very difficult to get in any house, in the Western world at least, where there isn't some kind of consumer product with the Dolby logo on it. You've never changed that image: where does the idea of the double-D logo come from?

Dolby: Well, the D comes from Dolby and the double D represents a symmetrical process, a mirror-image process, because that was the key to the success of my noise reduction system: that it was a perfect mirror image. In other words, you got out exactly the same signal that you fed into the beginning of the process, not something that is a little bit like it, or almost like it but not quite, exactly the same thing. You could show it mathematically, you could show it by tests using test signals and instruments, you could demonstrate it using music and listening with your ears. So it's a truly symmetrical system.

Sergi: Was it your choice to have the Dolby logo on all posters, or was it just something that happened?

Dolby: No. We wanted that, because we wanted to popularise the process and see it more widely used and we had already established that principle with the A-type tapes and everybody had to understand that if it was encoded with the process it had to be decoded with the process, and so we had labels and stickers and things like that that people could put on their tapes as being Dolby A-type encoded and so on. Then the process was further driven home when B-type came about. The consumers had to have some way of knowing whether they should push their Dolby button on the cassette that they bought. So we called the agreement that controlled our trademark the 'standardisation agreement' so that the trademark would be properly used and the type of process was correctly identified and also so that correct standards were maintained.

Sergi: [The year] 1977 in many ways was a turning point, a point where films like *Star Wars* and *Close Encounters of the Third Kind* come out, and they use Dolby technology and are a huge success.

Dolby: Yes, you should actually talk to Steve Katz if you really want to find out more about that, because he was the engineer who had the close contact at that time, and Ioan Allen of course. We just continued doing the same kinds of things with Lucas that we had been doing on any number of films that we had made up to that time.[9] Which meant going in there, showing the studios how to hook up our equipment, how to calibrate it, how to calibrate their own equipment, how to avoid certain mistakes or flaws in their own equipment that would impair the result, and just generally handle things. This was a lot of new stuff suddenly loaded on to people and they were very appreciative of having our help.

Sergi: After the release and success of the films we have just mentioned, did you think at that point 'OK, that's it now. It's not going to go away'?

Dolby: I've never lost the feeling that the whole world might come crashing down. I don't know, I think any time an entrepreneur thinks 'OK, I'm home and dry, I'm safe now' you're asking for trouble. I think *Star Wars* is grossly exaggerated in its effect, or significance; it was one of many steps along the way ... *A Star is Born*, that was a big hit, *Stardust* was a big hit, *Tommy* was a big hit, *Lisztomania* which was, I thought a wonderful film, we were very proud of that film – it had some wonderful piano recordings in it.

Sergi: What about the number of exhibitors who were 'convinced' by the success of *Star Wars* to install Dolby technology?

Dolby: If you look at the curves of films made per year it just keeps going up like this [he indicates an upward trajectory]. There were no big spikes or anything like that, just sort of a slow increase. That has characterised practically everything we have done. I don't know of any true breakthrough along the line. For example B-type licensing, we had to fight for every licensee, we had to fight for everything we did, pre-recorded tapes and things like that. We still have to fight. Again, you know, a successful company cannot rest.

Sergi: Is that why you then move on to Dolby Spectral Recording [SR] or was it in response to people asking for more?

Dolby: Well, in about 1974 the Philips company came to me in London, maybe it was 1975, and they had been using my professional system for some years, and they said 'we like your system but we want more noise reduction'. I expressed some scepticism whether more noise reduction was necessary. What I was really saying was 'God! That's going to be a horrible project, an immense project to do if it is to be done properly'. I just dreaded it because I had various ideas on how to make more noise reduction but I knew that it would require a lot of time and effort and I didn't get around to it until 1980 and it took six or seven years to create SR. I had to haul myself up again, the way I had done early on with the various designs and developments. The top floor of my home was turned into an audio and electronics laboratory. I couldn't do it at the company because people interrupted me all the time. I'd get sucked into this project or that discussion or this meeting or that meeting so I almost cut myself off from my company during the development of the C-type noise reduction system and SR.

Sergi: Why didn't anybody else, when they saw the kind of success you were having, try to do something similar?

Dolby: Oh they did. You had the Burwin company, you had the DBX company and others who tried to make noise reduction systems, but they, funnily enough, went back to use the old principles. They had forgotten about why the old principles didn't work and eventually they were found out and those systems disappeared.

Sergi: When did you get into digital?

Dolby: We started our digital work in the late seventies and throughout the eighties; Louis Fielder's work was in the late eighties I guess – mid- to late eighties. We knew about digital developments and we didn't want to get left too far behind so we produced our own digital or quasi-digital system, the so-called AC1 system, Audio Coder No. 1 system. It's a system that uses some digital techniques and some analogue techniques and that filled a certain technology slot. It's still being used in some places, but the pure digital embodiments began to take over and of course we joined that with our AC2 system, which Louis Fielder developed.

Sergi: What's the next step for you?

Dolby: There is no major next step. It's a matter of being constantly aware of one's environment, of keeping track of what's happening in the various industries we are operating in and sensing of what's possible, what's not possible, what's needed, what's not needed. It's having all your antennas going. I don't think you can say that there is one particular thing that you have to do next.

Sergi: Let me just ask a final question. In academic circles a lot of people would say that technology drives aesthetic choice. Other people might say that perhaps is more of a dialogue: the filmmakers come to you with a need and you respond to it. What's your view?

Dolby: I think there is an interaction and one party responds to the other, and I think the two parties try to optimise whatever they are doing. For example, let's say the audio equipment designer knows that if there is a very loud sound on the soundtrack, the soundtrack is going to overload and you are going to get a distorted sound and that's a bad thing, and so he tries to work out some new technology that will permit louder sounds to be recorded and the filmmakers see this and they say 'this is great, let's use this'. So the next thing you have is people complaining that movies are too loud and this has been a source of a lot of trouble for us. Before we allowed this very wide dynamic range, before it was possible to record these wide dynamic ranges, the filmmakers were kept in check because they knew that the sky wasn't the limit, there were limits to what they could do. But now people can make sound as loud as they want to in the theatre, and the young turks who are at the controls on the console think it's just so much fun to make a film that has real impact, a soundtrack that has real impact. So, you can't win. We are now doing a lot to try to get the sound levels down in movie theatres.

Sergi: Have you done any scientific research on this?

Dolby: I don't know whether we have done any scientific research. It's just more or less word-of-mouth kind of thing.

Sergi: What about audience attitudes to sound: have you ever tried to find out directly from audiences how important it is for them to have good sound in the theatres?

Dolby: I don't know whether we have done anything like that. I know that people, let's say, when given an improvement of some kind take a while to understand what the improvement is and to appreciate it, and so they may not say 'wow, this is great I love it'. They just get used to it, and then if you take it away from them, then that upsets them. For example air conditioning: who thinks about the value of air conditioning any more? You just take it for granted, but if it's a hot day and the air conditioning fails, every-body is very upset. Or you go into a restaurant and it's very hot, like the restaurant we were in at lunchtime, it was very warm in there [chuckles] and you just think 'well, they just can't afford an air conditioner I guess', so we are very aware when something good is taken away from us.

Notes

1 Alexander M. Poniatoff was a legendary figure in the field of audio engi-neering. He created what is now known as the AMPEX Corporation in 1944, and was behind the creation in 1948 of the Model 200, the first professional audio tape recorder (based on a German model that had been used during World War Two). In 1956 Poniatoff and other colleagues at AMPEX, including Dolby, created the first rotary head recorder, which made video recording a possibility for the first time.
2 Dolby was part of the team that worked on the first video tape recorder, the Mark IV at AMPEX.
3 Dolby studied for a PhD in Physics at the University of Cambridge (UK). In the last year of his study at Cambridge, he also acted as a

consultant for the United Kingdom Atomic Energy Authority. He later spent two years in India between 1963 and 1965 working as a United Nations Adviser to the Central Scientific Instruments Organization. On his return to England in 1965 he formed Dolby Laboratories.

4   Cyril Windebank and Bob Goodman were respected engineers at Decca for many years. Windebank was chief engineer at Decca at the time and Goodman was responsible for the creation in 1961, together with Roy Wallace, of the 'Mono and Stereophonic Electronic Recording Equipment' a 15-channel mixer that became known as MASPERE, an acronym of the mixer's initials.

5   The two systems being tested by Decca were from EMP and EMI.

6   The interview with Ioan Allen appears on page 91.

7   David Robinson has been with Dolby Labs since 1966. He is currently Senior Vice-President for Technology.

8   Avery Fisher and Hermon Hosmer Scott were two pioneers of radio. Avery Fisher is a legendary figure in the arts patronage (perhaps the most famous of Fisher's patronages is the Avery Fisher Hall at the Lincoln Center in New York). He was an inventor and founder of the consumer electronics company Fisher Electronics. Herman Hosmer Scott was famous for inventing the Dynaural Noise Suppressor, which helped to free radio stations from the constraints of live-only radio.

9   Steve Katz was the Dolby Consultant on many key films of that period, including *Star Wars*, *Close Encounters of the Third Kind* and *Days of Heaven*.

3

Critical receptions of sound

It is difficult to imagine how the auditory dimension of cinema might at this late stage be reinstated. (Rick Altman)[1]

Sound has traditionally inhabited the peripheries of film scholarship, apart from two extremely busy periods. The first concentrates on issues concerning the coming of sound in the late 1920s and 1930s. The other, of which this study is an example, has mostly been the product of interest generated from the mid-1970s onwards during the Dolby era, a period Charles Schreger intelligently referred to as 'the second coming of sound'.[2] Although there has been some interesting critical writing on film sound in the forty years between those two key moments, the split exists nonetheless. These two main 'splinters' of sound literature are less independent of each other than the time difference might suggest. Indeed, the quantity and kind of critical attention that the coming of sound has received over the decades, from early theorists such as Eisenstein, Kracauer, Arnheim and Bazin to the present day has had a profound influence on the way film sound has been researched, written on and taught until now. This 'time rift' is not the only peculiarity that any survey of film sound scholarship will reveal. There would seem to be a further, revealing split in the way attention to sound in the cinema has been documented. On the one hand, substantial accounts of film sound from traditional academic sources, be it in historical or aesthetic terms, are relatively scarce. This is especially true when playing this scarcity of material against the wealth of books on cinema currently available.[3] On the other hand, in recent years the rise of the Internet as a means to showcase views and 'histories' of film sound has proved a formidable force in liberating all those voices that had previously existed only in the underground of scholarly research due to their lack of 'proper' academic credentials. It is possible to index summarily the typologies of literature these two main groupings have produced:

1   Traditional accounts of sound (mostly generated by academics writing within the context of research publications for universities and colleges):
    *   Books and articles that have sound as their *raison d'être* (e.g. Rick Altman's *Sound Theory, Sound Practice*, and John Belton and Elisabeth Weis's *Film Sound: Theory and Practice*).
    *   Books where sound figures prominently (e.g. Steve Neale's *Sound, Color, Image*).
    *   Introductory books to film/cinema studies (e.g. Jill Nelmes's *An Introduction to Film Studies*, and Pamela Church Gibson and John Hill's *Oxford Guide to Film Studies*).
    *   Filmmaking manuals (the 'How to…' kind of book).
    *   Histories of cinema.
    *   Books on individual filmmakers.
    *   Film reviews (both in journals such as *Sight & Sound*, and in newspapers and magazines).
2   Novel accounts of sound (mostly the product of sound enthusiasts from a variety of backgrounds including, significantly, a large number of practitioners):
    *   Interviews with sound men and women (available through technical journals, such as *Mix* and *American Cinematographer*, on the Internet, and in other formats, such as the BBC Radio 4 four-part series on film sound, *Dancing Shadows*).
    *   Accounts of the use of sound in individual films (both on production and post-production, available in a variety of formats including the Internet, publicity material and, increasingly, on Laserdisc and DVD as extra material – see *Toy Story* or *Titanic* for good examples).
    *   Historical accounts of film (mostly on the Internet on dedicated sites to the history of sound and cinema reproduction, such as www.widescreenmuseum.com).
    *   Online articles on sound and sound journals (the best example of the former remains www.filmsound.org and www.cinemaaudiosociety.org; a good example of the latter is the Sound Journal run by the University of Kent at www.ukc.ac.uk/sdfva/sound-journal/index.html).
    *   Reviews of movies for home video magazines (video/DVD /Laserdisc).

On the one hand, despite a recent 'flurry' of books and articles on sound, the effects of decades of marginalising sound in academic contexts and discourses can still be deeply felt. The names involved (and invoked) are usually those of academics who have established their reputation in other, better-appreciated areas of film studies and have shown an honest attention to sound, mostly as a 'secondary' phenomenon (Bordwell and Thompson's efforts in this sense are perhaps the most obvious example). The exceptions, though noticeable (Altman and Chion), have often had to paddle upstream against the seemingly unstoppable current of thought that has championed the image as the true nature of cinema. Altman's heartfelt quote I mentioned at the beginning of this chapter is, in this sense, rather evocative. On the other hand, the sheer amount of writings on and around film sound that has appeared over the Internet and in 'technical' magazines is quite overwhelming. From countless accounts of aesthetic and technological contribution of individual filmmakers to a staggering drive for historical accounts of film sound in all its facets, this enthusiastic, at times crusade-like attitude of all those involved has developed a remarkable resource for scholars of sound and can now count on a steady readership.[4] Indeed, the rise of this 'novel' literature of sound is a further qualifying feature of the Dolby era for it highlights the political drive that some of Hollywood's leading designers have shown to leave the underbelly of film appreciation and establish themselves as 'artists', worthy of scholarly attention. Clearly, to attempt even a superficial account of all literature on sound would be as unfeasible and unwise a project as a similar enterprise on the image would be. I have therefore chosen to focus on some key aspects that emerge from existing sound scholarship both in relation to the way sound has been written about per se, and in terms of the 'place' that it has been assigned within film theory. In this sense, the most revealing place from which to begin is the influence that literature written nearly seventy years ago still has on film studies.

The sins of the fathers: the place of sound in film studies

Writing a foreword to the second edition of his book *Film as Art*, Rudolf Arnheim unequivocally states that 'Speech, wisely subordinated, supplements, explains and deepens the image; but the image continues to rule the screen, and to explore its properties remains a topical task'.[5] This is a reiteration of what he had written thirty years earlier, when he stated that 'No one who went unprejudiced to watch a silent film missed the noises which would have been heard if the same events had taken place in real life'.[6] Arnheim's distrust of sound comes from his difficulty in accepting that film as an audio-visual art form can function at all. He suggests that sound movies (he actually uses the expression 'talking' movies as he is mostly concerned with speech) give him a sense of uneasiness: 'It is a feeling that something is not right there: that we are dealing with productions which because of intrinsic contradictions of principle are incapable of true existence'.[7] In other words, Arnheim seems unable to accommodate the notion of two 'distinct media', as he sees them, working together effectively. His view of sound as a fundamental problem to the very existence and effectiveness of film as an art form is but one famous illustration of some of the prejudices that early theorists helped form and that subsequently hardened in film scholarship. In this sense, the position of most Russian formalists, such as Pudovkin and Eisenstein, helped reinforce a sense of distrust in sound. Their objection was one that revolved around the need, which they perceived as crucial to Soviet cinema, to go 'beyond' reality to reveal the real nature of the world. This could be achieved in a variety of manners. Montage, a practice that the formalist school intended as a way of combining images to produce or at least emphasise a 'message', was the key means of expressing the aesthetics of Soviet cinema. They argued that sound reinstated an element of reality that potentially threatened their aesthetic and political project (the two being inextricably linked). Although not all Formalists adhered to this view, Vertov being one of the most famous examples. Despite Eisenstein's acknowledgement of the potential of sound, provided that this could be used in an asynchronous and contrapuntal manner, the Russian school reinforced the notion of sound as being a hindrance to the image – indeed, a threat to filmmaking aesthetics.[8]

André Bazin would appear to have a different view of sound from other early theorists. The fundamental reasons for this difference is not so much a particular interest in sound but rather a realisation that the cause of realism is better served by the sound film and that, unlike Arnheim, Eisenstein and others, he believed that 'By 1928 the silent film had reached its peak'.[9] However, the problem Bazin runs into is not too dissimilar to Arnheim's: he eventually finds it difficult to overcome the separation of sound and the image as two separate entities. Although in a less virulent manner than in Arnheim's view, this inevitably gives rise to an impossible dichotomy whereby if it is not in film's nature to be an art form where sound and image work together harmoniously, then that true nature must be found either in the image or in the sound. Considering Bazin's emphasis on the importance of the photographic reproduction, this choice is really a false choice.

Bela Balasz offers a rather complex view of sound in his *Theory of the Film*.[10] On the one hand, he is adamant about the possibilities that sound might hold for the cinema. In a view that is in many ways diametrically opposite to Bazin's he claims that 'The demand is that the sound film should not merely contribute sound to the silent film and thus make it more like nature, but that it should approach the reality of life from a totally different angle and open up a new treasure-house of human experience.'[11] He goes on to assert that 'The asynchronous use of sound is the most effective device of the sound film'.[12] However, he still sees these only as possible future developments, whilst the certainty in his view is that sound killed silent cinema and in doing so reverted film to the much-dreaded 'filmed theatre': 'When the technique of the sound film struck the first blow at the art of the silent film, I said that it would destroy the already highly developed culture of the silent film ... I said that what had happened was a catastrophe, the like of which had never occurred before in the history of any other art ... On the whole the film has reverted again to a speaking photographed theatre.'[13] What appears unequivocally from these very influential early views of sound is that, despite their sometimes diametrically opposite understanding of what film is and what it could and should achieve, theorists of the early sound era saw the subordination of sound to the image as a necessity. Their inability to overcome the 'shock' of sound is nowhere more evident than in their discomfort at having to reconcile sound and the image. Ultimately, their choice to emphasise the separation of image and sound paved the way to half a century of image-biased film theory: for if sound and image cannot be reconciled in film, who would pick the former over the latter?

The introductory book syndrome: sound as an afterthought
In many ways, this false and damaging dichotomy is pervasive even in contemporary film literature. Perhaps the most revealing typology

of the kind of dismissive attitude scholars have often displayed about sound can be found in the 'introductory' type book. These books present themselves as a means for the uninitiated student and film enthusiast to begin their journey into greater appreciation of movies in all their complexity, they are thus a good indication of the 'status' of film sound amongst film scholars. A brief look at some of the most popular books of this kind is in this sense revealing. In *An Introduction to Film Studies*, edited by Jill Nelmes, sound is evoked in a couple of chapters. Chapter 4, 'Film Form and Narrative', written by Allan Rowe, deals with the aforementioned central issues of form and narrative. The heading with which he begins his chapter, 'Introduction: the act of viewing' is rather exemplary of the kind of bias at work here. Rowe eventually mentions sound, but he opens his account thus: 'The final element in constructing the "image" of a film is the soundtrack'.[14] In doing so he chooses to subordinate sound to the image from the word go. This is typical of the book as a whole. Overall, sound is present in little over 3 per cent of the total wordage. In Susan Hayward's *Cinema Studies – The Key Concepts*, the entry for sound/soundtrack occupies four pages (whereas, more logically, there is no such attempt to condense such a vast area in a single entry for the image).[15] The content of the sound entry is a brief description of the historical evolution of film sound, mostly in technological terms. Sound occupies 1 per cent of the book's total wordage. In *The Oxford Guide to Film Studies*, edited by John Hill and Pamela Church Gibson, there is a chapter on film music by Claudia Gorbman, one of the most active scholars in the field of sound.[16] Gorbman deals with the topic with ease and competency, but there is no mention of sound as a relationship of components, only music. Here one may argue that in an important sense sound actually does not figure at all in the book – but, even considering Gorbman's piece, sound covers just over 1 per cent of the total wordage. In Pam Cook's *The Cinema Book*, sound enters the frame in Cook's 'History of the Cinema' section.[17] Typically, sound is discussed under the heading of 'technology'. There is a total of two pages dedicated directly to sound, less than 1 per cent of the total wordage. Warren Buckland's *Teach Yourself Film Studies* presents us with another rather striking example of scholarly attitude towards sound. Although Buckland actually deals with sound in the chapter called 'Film Aesthetics', he continues to approach image and sound as two separate entities. Indeed, he waits until the last few pages of his chapter to proclaim that: 'Before we move on ... we can briefly look at sound'.[18] He then goes on to mention the concepts of diegetic and non-diegetic sound, as they were originally enunciated by Bordwell and Thompson (see page 63).

Within the 'surveying' or introductory book category there are examples of scholars who have tried a more serious analysis of the role of sound, or that have at least shown awareness of the 'sound issue'. There is an unusually interesting tension at work in James Monaco's *How to Read a Film*.[19] Despite following the usual pattern in dealing with sound as a technological issue in a section entitled 'Technology: Image and Sound', Monaco often warns against the risk of underestimating sound. He suggests that 'Ideally, the sound of a film should be equal in importance with the image'[20] and that 'Noise and effects are poor labels indeed for a worthy art'.[21] Although he never actually develops his 'doubts' into a proper argument for the reintroduction of sound in the way we learn about how movies function, Monaco shows a curiosity about sound that is often missing from introductory books. William H. Phillips's *Film: An Introduction* dedicates a chapter to sound and seriously attempts to discuss, if briefly, all component of a film's soundtrack.[22] Most importantly, however, he employs extracts from interviews with some practitioners in one of the rare attempts of this kind to bring in the element of practice. The obvious limitation in this sense is that Phillips does this only with music composers.

Victor Perkins's *Film as Film* presents us with a much more sophisticated and complex understanding of sound.[23] In particular, Perkins approaches sound as a further tool for the filmmaker, and one that cannot be separated by an understanding of its relationship with the image: 'Again, we are dealing with interaction: the image encourages us to accept the reality of the sound; the sound alerts our perception to particular aspects of the image'.[24] In considering images and sounds as inextricably linked, Perkins chooses to reject the dominant view that the relationship between sound and image is mostly a conflicting one. In his view, the 'definition of the image and the soundtrack as distinct formal elements was the source of the theorists' formal difficulty'.[25] However, within this acceptance of sound and image as tools for the filmmakers rather than separate entities constantly at war with each other, Perkins still appears to adhere firmly to a view of movies as dominated by images. Sound, because of its difficulty in being immediately recognised without its visual source, needs the image to provide audiences with 'an interpreta-tion' of it. Conversely, sound's role is that of directing our attention to specific aspects of the image. This notion is perfectly coherent within the theoretical framework Perkins adopts: film is as much about selection as it is about exclusion. Indeed, one act presupposes the other. In the understanding of this process lies the key to the interpretation of a filmmaker's work. Perkins's choice of sentence structure, as attentive as ever, reveals his attitude more than the sentence itself. Sound's role is clearly defined in subordination to that of the image. One might very well suggest the reverse of what Perkins suggests: sound encourages us to accept the reality of the image; the image alerts our perception to particular aspects of the soundtrack.

Undoubtedly, the account of sound in introductory books that has received the largest amount of appreciation and is most often referred to remains Bordwell and Thompson's in their book *Film Art: An Introduction*.[26] The chapter dedicated to sound, 'Sound in the Cinema', is an interesting and insightful attempt at grasping the basics of film sound. Their account remains mostly concerned with the production of meaning in movies and they analyse sound accordingly. To illustrate their point about how 'sound can actively shape how we perceive and interpret the image' they use an extract from Chris Marker's *Letter from Siberia*.[27] In it, Marker chooses to play back three times the same sequence of Soviet workers working during the harsh winter on some public work project in the city of Yakutsk. Each time a different commentary is laid over the image, each time 'producing' a different meaning. Bordwell and Thompson's analysis goes well beyond that, borrowing some key concepts from existing work on sound (the notes at the end of the chapter provide an excellent insight into the background to their analysis of the role of sound). There appears to be a serious attempt at creating some kind of vocabulary of key concepts. As well as the much-quoted concepts of diegetic and non-diegetic sound (the usefulness of which is actually rather limited due to their ambiguous meaning), Bordwell and Thompson discuss issues of 'creative choice' (with terms such as selection, alteration and combination) as well as film sound dynamics (exploring concepts such as rhythm and space).

However, when they move to their final section of their book that deals with sample analysis of some films, they seem curiously unwill-ing to incorporate sound in their account. One of the films they discuss is *Raging Bull*. Widely considered as one of the best examples of creative sound in Hollywood cinema, *Raging Bull* is primarily the work of the collaboration between one of the most highly respected Hollywood sound designers, Frank Warner, and director Martin Scorsese. The non-literal approach to sound in the movie, especially during the fight sequences, has a dramatic effect on the overall feel of the movie and the way it impacts on audiences. In particular, Warner and Scorsese's choice of designing the breathing of boxers as a combination of animal sounds played back at different speeds and mixed with other sounds conveys an eerie, unsettling quality to the fight scenes. The mixing of those sounds with the aggressive sounds of the camera flashes documenting the fights creates very effective contrasts between the very personal world the boxers inhabit when in the ring and the outside world's sadistic desire to witness their public humiliation. This latter point is reinforced by Warner and Scorsese's use of radio and TV adverts casually informing the public that somehow, in the midst of such personal moral and physical destruction the 'spectator' should be made aware of the fact that there is a new toothpaste in town. The sound orchestration in *Raging Bull* is as daring as it is inventive and effective. Yet, when describing the same fight sequences I have just summarily described, Bordwell and Thompson seem to focus solely on the visuals. Their account is worth quoting in full:

> Apart from the narrative structure, Scorsese puts Jake's violence in context by means of film techniques. In general, by appealing to conventions of realism, the film's style makes the violence in *Raging Bull* disturbing. Many of the fights are filmed with the camera on a Steadicam mount, which yields ominous tracking movements or close shots which emphasize grimaces. Back lighting, motivated by the spotlights around the ring, highlights droplets of sweat or blood that spray off the boxers as they are struck. Rapid editing, often with ellipses, and loud, stinging cracks intensify the physical force of the punches. Special makeup creates effects of blood vessels in the boxers' face spurting grotesquely.[28]

Aside from a rather non-descriptive reference to 'loud, stinging cracks', sound is not mentioned. The question here is: why? After all, as we have seen, Bordwell and Thompson amply demonstrate their ability to suggest ways in which a serious analysis of sound can be carried out in the examples they use in the chapter on sound. Their evaluation of the importance of sound is also rather unequivocal when they state that 'With the introduction of sound cinema, the infinity of visual possibilities was joined by the infinity of acoustic events'.[29] Why, then, should they revert to such a visually dominated kind of analysis in the final section of their book? In many ways, I am being unfair here. Bordwell and Thompson's treatment of sound is one of the most serious and best presented available in the 'Introductory' books. Where others, as we have seen, are simply satisfied with a customary side-glance, Bordwell and Thompson's attempt is substantially more engaging. However, precisely because of this, their failure in bridging good intention with actual action is symptomatic of a key problem that has hindered the development of any serious critical appreciation and understanding of film sound.[30] Despite good intentions, Bordwell and Thompson's account ends up reinforcing the widely held view that sound is a secondary force in film.

Most scholars have been unable or unwilling to take that all-important step that would help suture the artificial dichotomy of image versus sound. A clear legacy of early writings on cinema, where the coming of sound was overwhelmingly seen as calamitous for film aesthetics, sound has spent most of its life in a film 'ghetto'. Scholars have often paid homage to the importance and role of sound only then to disregard it entirely when addressing theoretical issues, analysing movies, writing histories of cinema and, significantly, shaping film studies curricula.[31] The basic common denominator that all the accounts above share – with the possible partial exception of Perkins, and Bordwell and Thompson – is a lack of interest in the creative process involved in film sound. The view that dominates all these accounts is one that sees sound either as a technical/technological enterprise, hence not belonging to the creative realm, or as something of a hindrance to the development of film art.

A category of lack: sound as 'incomplete'

Interestingly, this rather 'suspicious', if not hostile, attitude towards sound can often be found in books and articles that have film sound at the core. The main heading under which we can group this different category of literature on sound is the category of 'lack'. This could be summarised as work where the investigation of sound in terms of its potential for creativity is defined in terms of what is actually not doing, in terms of what it lacks. Scholars as different from each other as Michel Chion, Walter Murch, Mary Ann Doane, and John Belton, to name but a few, have contributed in different ways to this type of sound literature.[32] The 'dialogue' between Doane and Belton in *Film Sound: Theory and Practice* is exemplary in this sense.[33] Belton writes on the relationship between technology and aesthetics mostly in response to Mary Ann Doane's much quoted 'Ideology and the Practice of Sound Mixing', which immediately precedes Belton's chapter in the book. Doane argues that technological improvements in sound, such as Dolby technologies, have worked towards 'hiding' the apparatus. In Doane's view, technology has served an ideological function in attempting to eliminate any trace of the fact that whilst at the movies we are actually experiencing a construct, not a value-free representation of reality. In this, she echoes work done by French theorists, such as Comolli and Baudry, on the importance of what they call 'the ideology of the visible'. That is, the bourgeois notion that the world is as it looks, as opposed to, for example, being a class-dominated version of many possible alternatives (cinema, in its claim to being able to photograph reality impartially can therefore be logically understood as an instrument of bourgeois ideology).[34] Doane argues that the development of sound technologies and practices aimed at eliminating any evidence of artificial intervention and manipulation of what is recorded is another aspect of the ideology of the visible that she defines as a 'repression of the material heterogeneity of the sound films'.[35] She states that 'The rhetoric of sound is the result of a technique whose ideological aim is to conceal the tremendous amount of work necessary to convey an effect of spontaneity and naturalness. What is represented in this operation is the sound which would signal the existence of the apparatus.'[36] In other words, her argument revolves around what sound does not do: sound's specific lack here is the inability to reveal the work that would 'signal the existence of the apparatus' (hence of the presence of an ideological struggle). In what appears to be a direct response to Doane's argument, Belton would seem to react to this view by stating that: 'Technology and the effects of technology … remain visible, though to varying degrees, in every film. The work of sound technology, through its very efforts to remain inaudible, announces itself and, though concealed, becomes audible for those who choose to listen for it.'[37] However, Belton goes on to define sound once again in terms of what it lacks and cannot do: 'Sound lacks objectivity (thus authenticity) not only because it is invisible but because it is an attribute and thus incomplete in itself … What the sound track seeks to duplicate is the sound of an image, not that of the world.'[38]

Belton's argument appears to revolve around the inability of sound to represent the pro-filmic world. The advancements in technology (like Doane, he refers to Dolby and mentions *Raiders of the Lost Ark*) have resulted in sound that he defines as 'unnatural', to the point that 'one misses the rough, jittery camera movements, floor squeaks, and unmixed ambient sound of films like Jean Renoir's *La Chienne*'.[39] Belton here is unwilling to consider that his argument implies that the world recorded by the image is not constructed, nor does he acknowledge that the creative processes at work in choices concerning set design and screenwriting are not at all dissimilar from issues of sound design and mixing. This latter aspect in particular should inform any serious attempt to understand how sound works in creative terms for it exposes the artificial nature of the distinction between what the image does and sound does not. However, in these accounts ideology wins the day, and sound is relegated to matters of technology. It is useful to point out that this surprisingly ambivalent attitude to sound by sound scholars is not confined to the arguments above, but can also be found in what Rick Altman calls the 'ontological fallacy'.[40] This is just another example of the legacy left by early theorists who claimed that images without sounds could still be called cinema, whereas the inverse cannot be true. An obvious reaction to the introduction of sound, this view should have remained confined to the period when it was expressed, one of uncertainty and worry about the future of cinema. However, as Belton's case demonstrates, the ontological fallacy still informs so much writing on sound. Altman has perfectly encapsulated the element of 'surprise' at the persistence of such a view when he says that: 'Surprisingly, this dependence on ontological arguments comes not from the enemies of sound, but from its greatest defenders' and that 'A similar danger lurks in the work of Mary Ann Doane, Kaja Silverman, Michel Chion, Claudia Gorbman and other critics.'[41]

The case for both Michel Chion and Walter Murch deserves closer attention. Michel Chion has been one of the most outspoken theoreticians on sound. His work has indeed been fundamental to the development of a scholarship of sound. His accounts of the role and importance of sound in the cinema has provided a whole new generation of scholars with the basis from which to develop further individual studies of sound. In particular, Chion's work is important in two key aspects. Firstly, he was one of the first scholars to attempt to develop a basic vocabulary of sound with which to articulate thinking on and around film sound. Secondly, and perhaps more importantly, he has dared to suggest that sound has, especially in the period I am considering, challenged, often successfully, the primacy of the image. For instance, he claims that 'Today's multipresent sound has insidiously dispossessed the image of certain functions – for example, the function of structuring space'.[42] This has resulted, in his view, in more complex sound constructions. As far as my study is concerned, also of particular relevance is his view that 'The sound of noises, for a long time relegated in the attic, has therefore benefited from the recent improvements in definition brought by Dolby'.[43]

Despite the unquestionable relevance of his work, Chion also shows deep ambiguities about sound that ultimately threaten to undermine his work. These ambiguities are present in two key areas, namely the real status of sound (in relation to the image) and what it can actually 'do'. In the first instance, Chion would seem to be unwilling to 'go the distance': this produces anomalies in his views that translate in somewhat confusing statements. In the aforementioned paragraph, where he states that sound has dispossessed the image of some key functions, he also states that 'Although sound has modified the nature of the image, it has left untouched the image's centrality as that which focuses attention. Sound's quantitative evolution – in quantity of amplification, information, and number of simultaneous tracks – has not shaken the image from its pedestal. Sound still has the role of showing what it wants us to see in the image.'[44] This view sits rather uncomfortably with the previous assertion about the new role of sound in the Dolby period and exemplifies the ambivalence about quite how far one could claim that sound matters. Whilst Chion is obviously entitled to doubts, these are not articulated enough: he would appear to state that sound is important only to then proceed to clip the wings of his own statements by confirming sound's secondary role in relation to the image.

Similarly, in the case of what sound can actually achieve, both Chion and Murch, though speaking of the power of sound in the cinema as effectively as any theorist around, again end up defining sound mostly in terms of what it lacks. The most obvious example of this is provided by Chion's book *Audio-Vision, Sound on Screen* to which Murch wrote a foreword. In it, Murch states that: 'The possibility of re-association of image and sound is the fundamental stone upon which the rest of the edifice of film sound is built, and without which it would collapse'.[45] Interestingly Murch feels the need to state what is a relatively obvious truism: sounds without images do not make a movie, and in doing so, he reveals the traditional emphasis on the image, for who would need to claim the same with respect to the film image?

Murch's comments in Chion's book are also indicative of a certain attitude to value what it is not immediately obvious in a soundtrack, the concepts Chion defines as 'synchresis' and 'added value'. Murch suggests that

> The danger of present-day cinema is that it can crush its subjects by its very ability to represent them; it doesn't possess the built-in escape valves of ambiguity that painting, music, literature, radio drama, and black-and-white silent film automatically have simply by virtue of their sensory incompleteness – an incompleteness that engages the imagination of the viewer as compensation for what is only evoked by the artist.[46]

Once again, we are paradoxically in the presence of two of the key theorists and practitioners of film sound who define sound mostly in terms of what it ordinarily lacks. In many ways, the position they represent is similar to that of early theorists who feared that synchronous sound threatened to reduce film to a lesser version of the theatre. In other words, sound ordinarily lacks the complexity needed to elevate film as an art form. It is only when there is some 'added value', when 'synchresis' is achieved, that sound finally fulfils its function (one that, in any case, would still appear to be subordinate to the image). When Chion defines his take on the concept of the 'achousmatic' sound (a concept, describing a sound whose visual origin is not revealed, that was first employed by Pierre Schaeffer and the *musique concrète* movement), he suggests that 'Confronted with a sound from a loudspeaker that is presenting itself without a visual calling card, the listener is led all the more intently to ask, 'What's that?' (i.e. 'What is causing this sound?') and to be attuned to the minutest clues (often interpreted wrong anyway) that might help identify the cause.'[47] In other words, both Chion and Murch would appear to value sound in the cinema as an important creative tool, but only in a certain form and as functioning within a certain 'artistic' project. By narrowing down their approach so much, they are effectively excluding 'ordinary' use of sound as interesting, as well as mostly discounting the experience of the audience to which they so often refer. Indeed, who is the listener they refer to? This is important, because their argument would seem to ignore countless accounts, on the part of both audiences and sound people alike, that audiences react mostly in a hostile manner to 'achousmatic' sound (for more see my interviews with Bruce Stambler and Gary Rydstrom later in this book). Indeed, the presence of sounds whose function within the cinematic experience is not obvious is often mentioned as one of the most disrupting events in cinemas. Murch and Chion 'choose' to ignore this, and this renders their views and ultimately their view of film sound as rather dismissive of most mainstream cinema.[48]

A more positive approach: sound as a creative force

Despite the rather 'bleak' landscape that arises from the considerations above, it is important to note that there is a further dimension to traditional film research that has taken sound into account with a much more positive approach. Although this has manifested itself mostly through articles and chapters, whilst books remain a rarity, the late 1980s and 1990s saw some ground-breaking accounts of film sound appear.

From a historical perspective, the aforementioned *Film Sound: Theory and Practice* filled a gap in that it provided students of sound with an attempt at outlining the historical development of film sound criticism. The essays contained in the book, from early criticism to articles on Robert Altman and Dolby, have the merit of showing the many facets of the rather uneasy relationship that scholars have had with film sound. Weis and Belton's 1985 book is particularly relevant because, twenty years after its publication, it remains the most comprehensive of a handful of attempts at dealing with sound from a historical perspective that goes beyond the early sound period. Elisabeth Weis is also responsible for a number of very interesting and insightful articles on sound. In particular, her article 'Synch Tanks – The Art and Technique of Post-production Sound' is one of the best attempts at understanding the creative process involved in creating sound in relation to actual filmmaking practices (the word 'art' in the title speaks volume about Weis's stance).[49] Her attitude to investigating sound (she asks a very basic question: 'How does sound get on pictures?') drives Weis in the direction of filmmakers rather than, as is customary, towards other scholarly accounts of film sound. Indeed, her attempt to establish a 'dialogue' with professionals in the way she integrates material from interviews with sound men and women in her writing was mostly unprecedented in conventional film scholarship. This approach leads her to make two key assertions at the end of her article. She questions the role that directors play in creating sound when she says that 'Most directors, however, do not use the expressive potential of the soundtrack and leave sonic decisions up to their staff', and she then challenges the notion of sound personnel as 'technicians' by pointing out that 'The most respected sound designers and supervisors may be called technicians, but their artistry can be heard in all the films they touch.'[50]

The relevance of filmmakers' own experience and views about film sound had been, until that point, mostly the domain of technical books and journals. *American Cinematographer* and *Mix*, to name but two examples, had been running a relatively steady flow of interviews with creators of sound. However, despite these accounts and some excellent individual efforts, traditional scholarly publications had overwhelmingly neglected the enormous potential that talking to filmmakers could unlock.[51] Many excellent accounts of film sound technology, amongst which Barry Salt's *Film Style and Technology: History and Analysis*[52] and Steve Neale's *Cinema and Technology: Image, Sound, Color*[53] had investigated the relationship between technology and aesthetics, but had done so whilst firmly remaining within academia.

A key work in venturing into the world of filmmakers for inspiration came with Vincent LoBrutto's *Sound-on-Film: Interviews with Creators of Film Sound*.[54] A former practitioner in the field of film editing, LoBrutto had already written two books, which have at their core a serious attempt at understanding the creative nature of two other areas of filmmaking, film editing, and production design.[55] His attitude to all interviews is perfectly encapsulated in his opening salvo: 'The purpose of this book is to allow those who work in film sound to speak in their own voices about their art and craft'.[56] He also wisely chooses to interview people whose careers span virtually the entirety of the sound-on-film era, from Arthur Piantadosi (who started working for Warner Brothers in 1935 and won an Oscar for *All the President's Men*) and Frank Warner (whose career spans nearly fifty years and has almost mythical status amongst the film sound profession, having worked on movies such as *Spartacus*, *Taxi Driver* and *Close Encounters of the Third Kind*) to contemporary key figures, such as Gary Rydstrom (seven-time Oscar winner) and

Cecelia Hall (one of the few leading women in sound in Hollywood, winner of an Oscar for *The Hunt for Red October*). LoBrutto does not overlook the more traditionally well-known figures, such as Walter Murch (*The Conversation, Apocalypse Now, Godfather* trilogy), Ben Burtt (*Star Wars* trilogy, *Indiana Jones* trilogy, *ET*) and Skip Lievsay (*Goodfellas, Barton Fink, Malcolm X*).

Despite the importance of all the aforementioned scholars, no account of film sound scholarship, however incomplete, could bypass Rick Altman's body of work. Altman has undoubtedly been the most prolific and influential scholar on film sound within traditional film scholarship. The width and breadth of his work cover just about any aspect of film sound, and the special issue of *Yale French Studies, Cinema Sound*, dedicated entirely to film sound that he edited in 1980 is widely regarded as being one of the first steps in the life of contemporary film sound research. His most important contribution is arguably his 1992 book *Sound Theory, Sound Practice*.[57] Despite being a collection of essays – including work from Michel Chion, John Belton and James Lastra – the book is a showcase from some of Altman's most incisive and effective writing. Crudely, Altman's aim would seem that of 'complicating' traditional scholarly attitudes to sound. There is an invigorating sense of rediscovery in his writing: sound is more complex than we have thus far acknowledged and requires accordingly a more sophisticated approach. For brevity's sake, I would like to limit my account of Altman's work to a few key aspects that are of particular relevance to this study. In the introduction to the book, Altman speaks, amongst other things, about multiplicity, three-dimensionality and materiality. These three issues help build up a framework that is particularly useful. Steven Spielberg once remarked that to see *Close Encounters of the Third Kind* in 6-track sound was not just a different experience of the same film, it was like experiencing a 'different film'.[58] Altman treats this difference in release formats less as a technological curiosity, and more as evidence of the existence of multiple versions of a film. In doing this, he highlights that

> Critics have effectively neutralized much of cinema's complexity. In doing so, they have systematically concentrated on the uniformity of the image, thus neglecting such essential variations in the soundtrack as 1) three decades of live, un-standardized accompaniment of 'silent' films, 2) simultaneous release of silent and sound versions during the

late twenties and early thirties, and 3) parallel distribution of magnetic
and optical track versions during the fifties and sixties, as well as
mono, stereo, and surround versions in the seventies and eighties.[59]

This concept is of particular importance because it suggests that
our appreciation of a film soundtrack depends on conditions of
reception, something that most scholars and film critics alike continue to refuse to acknowledge.[60] Altman's emphasis here is clearly
shifting from text to reception and the space(s) of reception. He fur-
thers his argument when he discusses sound's three-dimensionality.
Unlike the image's two-dimensionality, 'sound cannot exist in a two-
dimensional context'.[61] Although Altman refers specifically to cinemas ('sound occurs only in the three-dimensional volume of the
theatre at large'), the implication is that we should review our system
of critical analysis to include this aspect. As a three-dimensional construct, sound needs a vocabulary and a conceptual framework for
analysis that allows for such complexity. Most film criticism revolves
around the understanding of cinema as a two-dimensional construct
(this in spite of the fact that film image attempts at creating the illusion of depth). Finally, the concept of 'materiality' points at another
crucial dimension of sound and of cinema at large. The implication
of what Altman argues is that by acknowledging the many 'events'
that contribute to the production, exhibition and reception of a film
we can begin to see the complex nature of cinema aural audienceship:

> Such an approach encourages us to move past the imaginary space of
> the screen to the spaces and sounds with which cinema must compete
> – the kids in the front rows, the air conditioner hum, the lobby cash
> register, the competing sound track in the adjacent multiplex theatre,
> passing traffic, and a hundred other sounds that are not part of the text
> as such, but constitute an important component of cinema's social
> materiality.[62]

The view from the trenches: filmmakers writing on sound

As I pointed out at the beginning of this chapter, there is a different
though related body of knowledge concerning film sound. It arises
from countless accounts of filmmakers' use of sound in individual
movies, historical accounts of the development of the art and technology of film sound, and interviews with the makers of movie soundtracks. Although technical journals and home video magazines have
provided an outlet in the traditional print format, it is the Internet

that has ultimately proven to be the real propulsion behind the exponential growth of interest in and around film sound. It is not just the
means of diffusion that makes Internet material worth looking at, but
also the mode of investigation and the language adopted. As I mentioned earlier, traditional scholarship revolves around theoretical discussions in the sense of topics discussed without much direct
reference to professional practices and film practitioners. The first
thing that is striking about this second body of knowledge is the
extent to which it relies on practitioners and on accounts of filmmaking practices. This manifests itself not only in terms of topics discussed, but, crucially, in the way practitioners are often the agents of
this literature of sound. One perfect example of this phenomenon is
Randy Thom. Responsible for the sound in films such as *Forrest
Gump*, *Arlington Road*, *Cast Away* and winner of an Oscar for Best
Sound for his work on *The Right Stuff*, Thom is rightly considered
one of the most experienced sound men in Hollywood. He is also a
prolific writer on matters relating to film sound. He writes on both
technical issues and aesthetic matters.[63] Thom's writing has mostly
raised questions around the issue of status for film sound and the
consequent lack of attention on the part of filmmakers. He argues
that a greater understanding of the demands of sound work, especially post-production sound, would greatly enhance the quality of
film. In particular, he highlights writers and directors as the two categories that can most benefit from thinking about sound more. In a
passage that is revealing of the general attitude of directors towards
sound in Hollywood, he says:

> Feature film directors tend to oscillate between two wildly different
> states of consciousness about sound in their movies. On one hand, they
> tend to ignore any serious consideration of sound (including music)
> throughout the planning, shooting, and early editing. Then they sud-
> denly get a temporary dose of religion when they realize that there are
> holes in the story, weak scenes and bad edits to disguise. Now they
> develop enormous and short-lived faith in the power and value of
> sound to make their movie watchable. Unfortunately it's usually too
> late, and after some vain attempts to stop a haemorrhage with a band-
> aid, the director's head drops, and sound cynicism rules again until late
> in the project's post production.[64]

Perhaps the best example of the insight into professional practices
that Internet material has provided scholars of film sound with is the
Open Letter from Your Sound Department.[65] It is a manifesto signed

by dozens of Hollywood's leading film men and women addressed to directors in which they outline the situation of production sound in filmmaking today (a vastly under-researched area within sound scholarship) and suggest ways in which this could be improved. As this revealing short passage indicates, the letter is an extremely useful resource in understanding how the image bias at work in film criticism is merely an extension of filmmaking practices:

> All of the other departments work for what is seen and not heard. Every single person on the production from make up and wardrobe to grips and props concentrates only on what's seen in the viewfinder. Because the other production crafts work only for picture, no one knows or cares what's happening to YOUR audio. You are the only person on set with the power to allow us to get you good sound. It is always tempting for sound to give in and not go against the grain when circumstances impose impossible barriers. Film schools are going to need to add psychology courses to their sound mixing curriculum soon. The situation is often that bad.[66]

What is the picture that arises from looking at existing work on sound? We still know very little in crucial areas such as how a soundtrack actually works, both internally and externally (i.e. in relation to the film's narrative and to its images). In historical terms, most accounts of sound have been limited to either the early sound period, or as a straightforward account of 'what was invented when'. Little has been done to try to understand how developments in sound have affected the industry as a whole, in financial, institutional, technological and aesthetic terms. Key areas that could potentially be revisited in light of greater attention to sound remain under researched: from genre to auteurism, from audience reception to performance the potential for further analysis is great indeed. When attention has been granted to sound, it has mostly been either in a marginal way or in a rather ambiguous tone.

There is a further aspect of this situation that has proven particularly damaging. Accounts of sound in the cinema have too often borrowed from established vocabularies in other disciplines rather than attempting to develop a more medium-specific framework. This is nowhere more evident than in the case of film music. Despite being one of the few areas of sound to have escaped the periphery of film scholarship (several studies of film music and individual composers have been published over the years), film music can actually provide us with an insight into the ways in which the lack of a conceptual and linguistic framework to investigate film sound continues to curb film research today.

A point in case: music in film and film music

Music is one area of film sound that has received a considerable amount of critical attention. Scholars such as Claudia Gorbman, Jeff Smith, Kaja Silverman, Kevin Donnelly and many others have explored its potential, reviewers have acknowledged its influence, and historians have mapped composers' efforts and their lives. Hence, it would be logical to assume that it should be possible to investigate film music with a certain degree of sophistication. There ought to be a set of linguistic and conceptual tools available to scholars to probe all aspects of film music: how it works, its relationship with sound effects and dialogue, the working practices that regulate its use, and so forth. Unfortunately, this is far from being the case.

I would like to begin with a 'simple' question: why has film music recently enjoyed such a considerable amount of interest whilst other aspects of film sound have been regularly disregarded? Since the inception of audio-visual shows that could be identified in some ways as precursors of the cinema (such as the theatre, magic lantern shows and opera), sound agency has been firmly kept behind drawn curtains, 'hidden' away in an attempt to avoid distracting the audience.[67] Indeed, in plays, operas and early film shows the sound effects artists were kept at a safe distance from the audience's eyes.[68] This practice has often been interpreted as satisfying the need for maximising the sense of audience involvement in the fiction at play, be it a realistic piece of filmmaking or a fantastic reproduction of a journey to the moon. However, the practice of hiding sound agency has not been universally applied to all aspects of sound. Whilst effects troupes were kept firmly away from the audiences they performed for, musicians were often proudly displayed. A clear legacy of the status that music enjoyed in aristocratic circles throughout Europe for centuries, the display of orchestras and solo musicians has always been seen as an integral part of the show, hence the desire to showcase it. Musicians cannot distract an audience from the show simply because they are part of the show. The ultimate consequence of this practice has been a separation of music and sound effects as belonging to two different areas: the artistic (music) and the technical (sound effects). The former is to be proudly displayed; the latter is to be dealt with 'as quietly as possible'. This separation, and the connotations that it brings with it, is also 'justified' by a key consideration. It is much easier to identify agency in the case of music than sound effects. In the world of aristocracy there were men of letters, playwrights, musicians and painters. That is, men and women working alone. In this sense the figure of the composer provided a clear and obvious opportunity to praise individual genius.

A false dichotomy: the 'purist' approach

Perhaps unsurprisingly, this whole set of expectations and attitudes has been carried on to the appreciation and investigation of movies. This can be partly explained by the fact that some of Hollywood's most successful composers (such as William Korngold, Max Steiner and Alex Newman) had a classical background and often showed clear signs of its influence in their music scores. This, as Jeff Smith reminds us, added a certain air of respectability to what was otherwise regarded as 'second-class music': 'Romanticism added a High Art sheen to the work of Hollywood film composers. This not only elevated film music in the eyes of film producers, it also enhanced Hollywood composers' own claims of authorship and creativity.'[69] This artificial separation based on the dichotomy art vs. technology and artist/auteur vs. technician is still very influential in contemporary film criticism. Indeed it has contributed in a substantial way to distort the kind of attention that we have given to film sound in general, and music in particular, and warrants a closer look at the critical approach that this situation has engendered. For argument's sake, I shall refer to this as the 'purist approach'. A first feature of the purist approach is to see the terms 'music' and 'soundtrack' as interchangeable. There are, of course, precise reasons to explain why this should be the case. Historically, film music scores have been marketed as the 'movie original soundtrack' or a variation on this theme. Often composers themselves have referred to their scores as 'the soundtrack' in interviews. Reviewers and scholars also routinely identify the music score as the soundtrack to the effect that the distinction between the two terms becomes invisible and to talk about the former satisfies the need to cover the latter. This has obvious consequences. To negate difference between the 'music score' and the 'soundtrack' is to suggest that the isolated study of the former will offer answers as to how the latter works. In other words, listen

to John Williams's score for *Saving Private Ryan* and you will be able
to suggest how the film's soundtrack works. This also extends to
whether we evaluate that film's soundtrack to be 'good' or not.
Indeed, if we were to view the music score as aurally isolated from
its context we would rightly be entitled to assess a composer's effort
in isolation, without further probing of all the other elements that
might influence our perception of his/her music.

This critical stance, adopted by most film scholars, has some obvious advantages. It favours the concentration of scholarly attention
on one figure (i.e. the composer) thus simplifying research, for it
would clearly take a much greater effort to investigate the web of
relationships at the core of film sound. Most importantly, it vouches
for a theoretical construct aimed at validating film as worthy of artistic and academic attention. The presence of an 'author', the inscrip-
tion of meaning in the film as text, and the availability of means
(namely, textual analysis) to reveal such meanings are all compatible
with the purist approach. This is a fundamental role: film as Art has
always seemed to tread a very fine line between tolerance and heresy
amongst art critics and academics alike, hence the political importance of anything that might confirm the validity of film as an object
worthy of study. As Richard Dyer suggests: 'The power of auteurism
resided in its ability to mobilize a familiar argument about artistic
worth and, importantly, to show that this could be used to discrim-
inate between films. Thus, at a stroke, it both proclaimed that film
could be an art (with all the cultural capital that this implies) and
that there could be a form of criticism indeed, study of it.'[70] Evidently, the purist approach serves at least one key function: its focus
on music rather than on the soundtrack and on the composer as its
sole auteur can be fully reconciled with the auteurist position. It
reaffirms both the validity of films as an object of study (especially in
its emphasis on high art) and of traditional textual analysis as the
valid method to carry out its investigation. In many ways, the very
existence of the notion of auteurism tends to direct scholarly attention to individual agency rather than collective effort and to the
established vocabulary of music analysis rather than the uncharted
waters of film sound appreciation. Indeed, Claudia Gorbman comes
very close to actually spelling out the auteurist nature of film music
scholarship when she points out that 'Within the general field of film
studies, the study of film music might well represent the last bastion
of film aesthetics'.[71]

When all the implications of this view are taken into account the result is a position that can be summarised in three key points. Firstly, the purist approach vouches for the validity of the distinction between the artistic and the technical in movies. Secondly, it sees the terms 'music' and 'soundtrack' as interchangeable and fundamentally meaning the same thing. Finally, it firmly posits responsibility and agency in the hands of the composer. However reassuringly familiar this notion of film music might be, we nevertheless need to ask a key question: does this approach help us ask the most useful questions when investigating film music? The purist approach would seem to be more interested in music per se than in the relationships music enters when being composed, mixed and reproduced for the cinema. Although this is perfectly understandable, it also means that some key aspects of film music and its role in the cinema have been either insufficiently researched or altogether neglected precisely because of this lack of attention to the specificity of the film medium. These neglected areas cover all the major facets of film music: how it is composed, how it is used in the context of the soundtrack, and how it is reproduced and received in cinemas.

The dynamic duo: music score and music in film

Film music does not work in a vacuum. Its function, and ultimately its rate of success, is inextricably linked to its greater whole, one that includes sound effects and dialogue. This relatively straightforward suggestion eludes the purist approach because of its tendency to identify the terms music and soundtrack as synonyms. To begin to overcome this limitation it might be useful to divide the expression 'film music' into two distinct terms: 'music score' and 'music in film'. The former will identify the score as it is marketed by the music industry. To use the example of *Saving Private Ryan* once again, John Williams's complete score for the film as marketed on a CD is that film's music score. The latter term, music in film, will refer to music as it appears in the final mix (that is, once it has been edited and mixed with sound effects and dialogue).

In contemporary filmmaking, these two 'versions' of film music are often separate though related entities. Crudely, a composer will most likely put together a 50-minute/70-minute score for any given movie. Often other music is added to the music score in the form of existing or purposely composed popular songs, before this is

packaged and marketed. However, only a percentage of that score
will end up in the final film soundtrack (indeed, it is not entirely
uncommon for the soundtrack to feature only a small percentage of
the originally composed score). The reason is simple: film soundtracks need to accommodate music, sound effects and dialogue. In
short, all the elements of a soundtrack, including music, need to be
mixed according to the needs of the whole, not the particular.[72]
    These three aural elements will have to share the physical limita-
tions of sound. The spectrum audible to humans is roughly between
20 Hz and 20,000 Hz (the higher the frequency, the higher the
tone). If sound designers and supervising sound editors were to
employ routinely a fully orchestrated piece of music without paying
attention to the context in which music is being employed, there
would most likely be no room left for any other sound, be it dialogue
or sound effects.[73] This is not merely a technological issue – aesthetic
choices are informed by technology, as sound designer Gary Rydstrom points out: 'Often the composer, the sound editor, and the
sound effects people in particular end up competing for any given
scene ... then in the mix you meet this big collision. A lot of time in
the mix is spent trying to figure out how we can feature music here,
feature sound effects there – how we can blend the two.'[74] A composer's first consideration will be for the narrative dimension of
music. However, he or she will also need to be aware of the articulate sonic structure in which his or her music will have to fit. To put
it differently, film composers find themselves in a position unlike
that of music-only composers. Although composing from similar
repertoires, film composers will have to confront a series of 'external factors' that will ultimately determine both how their music is
employed and how it is received by audiences. Thomas Newman's
score for *Erin Brockovich* might stand in its own right as 'good
music'. However, Newman's awareness of the context in which his
music is to be used has a fundamental influence in his style of composing. In a film where dialogue plays such an important role and
where the silences between sentences are just as important it
becomes crucial to have a score that will take all that into account
and 'blend' in rather than take over. Newman carefully arranges the
kind of frequencies his music covers so that dialogue and silence are
not 'drowned' by the music score. Similarly, John Williams's scores
for the opening of *Star Wars* and *Superman* are a perfect example of
when composers have carte blanche in relation to frequency and

thus can freely choose to go 'full-throttle' to inject pace and rhythm to title credits: this is a 'big' movie and I want you to know it from the word go whilst credits are still running.[75]

All this points to one consideration: in movies, the context in which music is employed is more articulate than in the case of the music medium. Whereas music is both content and medium in the music industry, this is not the case in the cinema: film composers will always have to refer to specific reference points, both in creative and technological terms, which are outside of their direct control. Music purists have often regarded this as a limitation to composers' artistic expression, in what is often a reiteration of the elitist nature of the purist approach. Darby and DuBois, for example, state that 'Film music is (further) affected by the ways in which it is added (or 'mixed') with dialogue and sound effects. All too often a composer's hard work must be truncated or submerged, if not lost altogether because of the demands of what are perceived to be more important elements ... such conditions can grate on composers.'[76]

If we are willing to accept that music in film is not 'the film's soundtrack' but one of its elements, we can begin to assess the role that it plays in contemporary soundtracks. A first consideration in this sense might sound harsh: music is rarely the structuring element of a soundtrack. Ask any sound professional in the business today what is the most important element in a soundtrack and you will almost invariably receive the same answer: dialogue. Today, as it has been since the inception of talking dialogue in movies, the principal preoccupation of filmmakers is to 'get the dialogue right' (i.e. clear and audible), as sound designer Bruce Stambler reiterates: 'I think you should hear all the dialogue. In a movie you are trying to tell a story. The first thing you think if the dialogue can't be heard is "I didn't hear what they said" and now you are no longer in the movie, period. You need to suck them in and keep them in.'[77] Despite the enormous improvements in sound technology since the 1980s and the remonstrations of many film composers, film sound is still very much centred on the voice.[78] Sound effects and music play key roles, but they are usually secondary to the dialogue. This is not to belittle the role that music or sound effects play within the soundtrack, but to highlight the collaborative nature of the process. This is particularly important when it comes to identifying agency and responsibility in contemporary film music. In particular, the issue of agency is very intriguing because it does not lend itself to pigeonholing.

How can we to tell who is actually responsible for the way(s) music functions in a movie? What are the criteria we should follow to identify a sonic 'author'? Perhaps more to the point, is it useful to even attempt such an enterprise? If we were to look back at the purist approach, the assumption is that we already know the answer to those questions: the sonic 'author' in movies is the music composer. The argument to back this up is that he or she is the only recognisable 'artistic figure' amongst a group of technologically minded craftsmen and -women. This view is so deeply rooted in our understanding of film sound as to be shared by most filmmakers themselves, as this appeal to reason by a leading sound designer indicates: 'The main attitude people have to change is that sound is a technical part. People think of it as negative cutting, it's the technical step at the end where you put the door slam, the cat meow, the traffic in – then you have a finished film.'[79]

The realities of filmmaking practices present us with a rather more complex and articulated picture than the one implied in conventional accounts of film music and the soundtrack. To begin with, the actual involvement that composers have with a film varies considerably according to factors such as composers' own working practices, the relationship that is established with the director and the sound crew, the time allocated to post-production, and so forth. Most composers will have little contact with sound designers and supervising sound editors in the crucial stage of the creation of the final mix (i.e. when the soundtrack is finalised and all the aural components are 'locked' together). Rarely will a composer discuss his or her choices with the sound team, and even more rarely will he or she be present at the final dubbing stage to monitor the use that sound designers, directors, film editors and even producers will make of his or her carefully composed music score. Once the music score is handed over to the director and the post-production team the role that the composer plays is significantly reduced. There are of course exceptions (for example the relationship between Ennio Morricone and Sergio Leone, or that between John Williams and Steven Spielberg), but these are more due to the special relationship that exists between director and composers who have worked together over a long period of time rather than the rule.

Thus, the music score undergoes a series of changes, such as editing and mixing, that are a direct result of the cooperation between the sound team, the editorial team and the director, but from which the composer will mostly be absent. This is the stage when the composer's music ends its life as 'music score' (to continue its commercial life in a reincarnation on the music industry stage) and becomes music in film, that is, part of the soundtrack. Once this web of interactions is taken into account, how could we reach a definitive conclusion as to who is actually responsible for the way music functions within any given soundtrack? We know who composed the music. We can find out who edited it and whether he or she added any significant amount of extra material. Next, we can investigate which place the music was given in the soundtrack by the sound designer and those who re-recorded it. We can even ascertain as to how well versed in all things sound the film director was. Finally, we can find out how efficiently the editorial machine worked to ensure a smooth progress in the final mix. The deeper we go, the more obvious it becomes that, although we can place the paternity of the music score in the hands of the composer, the same cannot be said of music in film. This is simply because there is a considerable number of people who can legitimately claim a share of the creative investment that goes into devising and employing music in film. These considerations are particularly important in relation to issues of reception. Film audiences will perceive music not as a separate entity but as part of a whole. In other words, once they are mixed together, the separate elements of the soundtrack will be inextricably linked and audiences' perception of them will be coloured accordingly. As John Williams eloquently points out, 'Well, concert music requires 100% of the intellectual and aural attention from the audience. But in a film we (composers) have to understand that we've got maybe 20% of the audience's attention and our role is to support the other aurally-prepared materials of dialogue and SFX the other 80%.'[80]

One example might help to illustrate further these key points. Take the case of a romantic piece of music. Music media audiences will perceive the phrasing and mood of the piece based on its musical qualities and conventions. That is, bar factors external to a normal listening environment or situation (such as personal circumstances), they will perceive that piece as 'romantic'.[81] Now consider the possibility that that same piece might be used in a soundtrack, perhaps to underscore a particularly romantic moment in the film. Picture the scene if you will. The two leads are sitting on the porch professing their love for one another. It is a quiet summer evening, and a light breeze occasionally rattles the wind chimes hanging from the ceiling producing a gentle tinkling sound. A distant sound of crickets and the occasional car passing by complete the soundtrack for this scene. In this context, film audiences will most likely perceive the music in a similar fashion as the music-only listeners: all elements of the sound-track work towards the same goal, the representation of a romantic situation. Let us now imagine a similar scenario but with a few aural changes. We will retain the music, the romantic leads, the porch and let us throw in the warm summer evening too. We then increase the sound of nearby traffic. The breeze is now playing up with a window that has been left ajar. As a result, there is a constant, almost rhyth-mic, noise of the window slamming against its frame. In the distance, we hear some people shouting whilst having a heated argument (maybe another couple arguing?). In this second scenario, whilst the visuals, dialogue, general set details and even the music may be the same, the other elements of the soundtrack work to suggest some-thing rather less idyllic about the two romantic leads and their situa-tion that in the previous example. More specifically, this is emphasised by the juxtaposition of sound effects and romantic music. I do not wish to suggest the musical qualities of the music piece have changed, but that the way music functions within the soundtrack and the way audiences will perceive and understand it have indeed been radically altered. Once again, these considerations emphasise the need to investigate the roles and importance of the other figures involved in the manipulation and representation (literally) of film music beyond the composer. Music editors, sound designers and re-recording mixers all have an input in the process that intervenes between a composer handing in the music score for any given film and the soundtrack being reproduced in a movie theatre.

The need for a 'medium-specific' approach

The focus on composers and music can rely on a well-established and documented history of traditions. This aids the 'framing' of crit-ical approaches to 'film music as music'. In this sense, discourses on and around tradition are instrumental in vouching for the validity and worthiness of the object of study. Hence, Sam Mendes's success is emphasised as being in the tradition of Orson Welles, Nora Ephron's writing and directing endeavour is in the tradition of Frank Capra's feel-good movies, and so forth. Although tradition is often invoked in the case of acting, directing, cinematography and composing, this has rarely been the case for sound.[82] In other words, tradition has been used in critical discourses to drive a wedge between the artists and the technicians: composers and cinematographers as artists, film and sound editors as technicians. This reference to identifiable traditions and models is not necessarily damaging to critical studies of cinema. However, the lack of attention to the specific nature of film music has hindered the development of an articulated position on film sound tradition(s). As a result, most work on film sound oscillates between histories of technological development on the one hand, and accounts of the work of individual sound men and women on the other. This is an issue of attitude as much as critical acumen. Two groups have mostly conducted the debates on and around film music: music scholars and composers themselves on the one hand, and film scholars with little or no direct investment in sound on the other. The first group shows characteristic signs of tension between the desire to investigate film music as another facet of music, and the hierarchy at work in music criticism that regards film music as 'less important' than 'serious' music.[83] Ennio Morricone captures this latter aspect in these starkly aggressive words: 'I don't want to do those [film music concerts]. I want to do non-film music, meaning more refined, difficult music.'[84]

The second group is genuinely concerned about providing an overview of film in all its aspects, and this necessitates some degree of attention to sound. However, the latter almost invariably focuses on music to the detriment of any serious attempt to investigate film sound. In many ways, the result is further confirmation of the original doubts about the role of sound in the cinema that early theorists had cast: you either see or hear. That is, musically trained scholars can talk about film sound but not images, traditionally trained film scholars are in a antipodal position: they can see but not hear. Gorbman has perfectly encapsulated this in a provocative remark: 'I suspect that once scientists have succeeded in mapping and explaining the brain, it will become clear that people who are film critics exercise different areas of the brain from people who can talk articulately about music they hear.'[85] We have not looked hard enough into key issues such as the relationships between music, sound effects and dialogue. We have not yet even begun to investigate the dynamics of audience reception of music specifically designed and recorded for film exhibition, nor have we attempted to look into related issues such as the design of cinema loudspeakers and their placement. Most importantly, we have not yet put enough questions to practitioners about the creative, technological and personal relationships that dictate the creation of film soundtracks.

Notes

1 Rick Altman, 'The Evolution of Sound Technology', in Weis 1985, p. 45.
2 Charles Schreger, 'The Second Coming of Sound', *Film Comment* (Vol. 14, Issue 5, 1978) pp. 34–37.
3 A quick survey with Amazon, the world's largest bookseller, reveals that there are over 9,000 volumes with the words cinema or film in the title in the entertainment section alone.
4 The web site www.filmsound.org (accessed 1 August 2003) is a case in point because it currently attracts over 30,000 discrete visitors every month, a huge figure given the specialised nature of the site.
5 Rudolph Arnheim, 'Foreword', in *Film as Art* (Berkeley, Los Angeles and London: University of California Press, 1971).
6 Rudolph Arnheim, *Film* (London: Faber & Faber, 1933) p. 33.
7 Arnheim, 1971, p. 199.
8 Indeed, synchronicity of sound and image was identified early on by some theorists as one of the most threatening aspects of sound.
9 Bazin, André *What is Cinema*, trans. Hugh Gray (Berkeley, Los Angeles and London: University of California Press, 1967), p. 23.
10 Balasz, Bela *Theory of the Film* (New York: Arno Press and the New York Times, 1972 [1952]).
11 *Ibid.*, p. 197.
12 *Ibid.*, p. 218.
13 *Ibid.*, pp. 194–195.
14 Jill Nelmes, *Introduction to Film Studies* (London: Routledge, 1999) p. 113.
15 Susan Hayward, *Cinema Studies – The Key Concepts* (London: Routledge, 2000).
16 Claudia Gorbman, 'Film Music', in P. Church Gibson, and J. Hill, (eds.), *The Oxford Guide to Film Studies* (Oxford: Oxford University Press, 1998), pp. 43–50.
17 Pam Cook, *The Cinema Book* (London: British Film Institute, 1999), pp. 2–57.
18 Warren Buckland, *Teach Yourself Film Studies* (London: Hodder & Stoughton Educational, 1998), pp. 19–20.
19 James Monaco, *How to Read a Film* (Oxford: Oxford University Press, 2000).
20 *Ibid.*, p. 125.

21 *Ibid.*, p. 213.
22 William H. Phillips, *Film: An Introduction* (Basingstoke: Palgrave Macmillan, 2002).
23 Victor Perkins, *Film as Film* (New York: Penguin Books, 1972).
24 *Ibid.*, p. 95.
25 *Ibid.*, p. 37.
26 David Bordwell and Kristin Thompson, *Film Art: An Introduction* (New York: McGraw Hill, 1993).
27 *Ibid.*, pp. 29–34.
28 *Ibid.*, p. 433.
29 *Ibid.*, p. 295.
30 The other two films they discuss, *Meet Me in St Louis* (1944) and *Tout va bien* (1972) also have interesting soundtracks, which, at least in the latter case, Bordwell and Thompson actually mention, but their account of sound remains marginal.
31 In this sense, most writing on the coming of sound served the double purpose of both celebrating the birth of sound whilst emphasising in the same breath the subordinate nature of sound to the image.
32 Walter Murch is a multi-Oscar-winning sound designer (*The Conversation*, *Apocalypse Now*, *The English Patient*) and one of the fathers of contemporary film sound. He has also published a number of theoretical pieces on sound and it is under this guise that I am including him in this list.
33 Belton and Weis (eds.) 1985.
34 For an excellent critique of the 'visual bias' present in most French theorists, such as Comolli and Metz, see Roy Armes, 'Entendre, c'est comprendre: In Defence of Sound Reproduction', *Screen* (Vol. 29, Issue 2, spring 1988), pp. 8–22.
35 Mary Ann Doane, 'Ideology and the Practice of Sound Mixing', in Belton and Weis (eds.) 1985, pp. 54–62.
36 John Belton, 'Technology and Aesthetics of Film Sound', in Belton and Weis (eds.) 1985, p. 61.
37 *Ibid.*, p. 63.
38 *Ibid.*, pp. 64–66.
39 *Ibid.*, p. 67.
40 Altman 1992, p. 37.
41 *Ibid.*, p. 38.
42 Michel Chion, *Audio-Vision, Sound on Screen* (New York: Columbia University Press, 1994), p. 144.
43 *Ibid.*, p. 155.
44 *Ibid.*, p. 155.
45 Walter Murch, 'Foreword', in Chion 1994, p. xix.
46 *Ibid.*, p. xix.

47 Chion 1994, p. 32.
48 In the case of Walter Murch, the appropriation of discourses of art typ-
    ically reserved to more established areas of filmmaking could be seen as
    a political attempt to 'talk up' the importance of his job as sound
    designer.
49 Elisabeth Weis, 'Synch Tanks – The Art and Technique of Post-produc-
    tion Sound', *Cinéaste* (Vol. 21, Issue 1–2, 1995) – supplement 'Sound
    and Music in the Movies', pp. 56–61. The article is also available
    online at: www.geocities.com/Hollywood/Academy/4394/sync.htm
    (accessed 1 October 2002).
50 *Ibid.*, p. 61.
51 Two excellent examples in this sense are Mark Mancini's 'Sound
    Thinking', *Film Comment* (Vol. 19, Issue 6, November/December
    1983), pp. 40–47 (which includes interviews with some key sound
    men, such as Frank Serafine, Ben Burtt and Jimmy MacDonald), and
    the special issue of *Film Comment* (Vol. 24, Issue 5, September/Octo-
    ber 1978), which has a special section on sound.
52 Barry Salt, *Film Style and Technology: History and Analysis* (London:
    Starword, 1983).
53 Steve Neale, *Cinema and Technology: Image, Sound, Color* (London
    and New York: Macmillan, 1985).
54 Vincent LoBrutto, *Sound-on-Film: Interviews with Creators of Film
    Sound* (Westport, CT: Praeger, 1994).
55 They are, respectively, Vincent LoBrutto, *Selected Takes: Film Editors
    in Editing* (New York and London: Greenwood Press, 1991), and Vin-
    cent LoBrutto, *By Design: Interviews with Film Production Designers*
    (New York and London: Greenwood Press, 1992).
56 LoBrutto 1994, p. xi.
57 Altman 1992.
58 La Polla 1982, p. 8.
59 Altman 1992, p. 45.
60 A greater appreciation of the condition under which a film is seen or
    heard would, for example, draw attention to the practice of reviewing
    new films in substandard theatres or on video. This practice has been
    one of the most important factors contributing to film criticism's virtu-
    ally complete lack of attention to sound, with the noticeable exception
    of music.
61 Altman 1992, p. 5.
62 *Ibid.*, p. 6.
63 A collection of his essays can be found in what is probably the largest
    single depository of articles on film sound, a web site run by a Swedish
    academic, Sven Carllson, www.filmsound.org (accessed 1 August
    2003).

64 Randy Thom, 'Designing a Movie for Sound', available at www.
filmsound.org/articles/designing_for_sound.htm (accessed 1 September 2002).

65 John Coffey, 'An Open Letter from Your Sound Department', available at:
www.soundspeedmovie.com/resources/articles/coffey/openletter.html
(accessed 1 September 2002).

66 *Ibid.*

67 It is worth pointing out that his pervasive concept of employing sound
in an 'invisible' way to avoid distracting the audience continues to be
the governing principle in contemporary sound design. It is also one of
the principle notions informing critical writing on film sound, as
employed by scholars such as Mary Ann Doane and Claudia Gorbman.

68 These artists were not an impromptu, disorganised bunch. The sound
effects trade was a profitable one at the beginning of last century with
troupes of sound effects makers touring the country providing effects
for plays and silent movies. For an interesting account of this early
stage of sound effects in the cinema, see Stephen Bottomore, 'An International
Survey of Sound Effects in Early Cinema', *Film History* (Vol.
11, Issue 4, 1999), pp. 485–498.

69 Jeff Smith, *The Sounds of Commerce – Marketing Popular Film Music*
(New York: Columbia University Press, 1998), p. 6.

70 Richard Dyer, 'Introduction to Film Studies', in Hill and Church
Gibson (eds.) 1998, p. 5.

71 Gorbman, 1998, p. 43.

72 It makes perfect commercial sense, of course, to have a music score to
market as a distinct and 'fuller' entity than the music as heard in the
movie. This can translate into a crucial differentiation of the product
(i.e. something 'original') whilst retaining some of the elements that
appealed to the general public in the first instance (e.g. a central
theme).

73 The blurring of the difference between the two roles of the sound
designer and supervising sound editor suggests that it is acceptable to
use the term sound designer to indicate both.

74 LoBrutto 1994, p. 232.

75 I do not wish to discount the rather creative use of text in the opening
credits of both *Superman* and *Star Wars*, but I wish to emphasise the
impact that sound has on the first few opening minutes of those movies.

76 William Darby, and Jack DuBois, *American Film Music* (Jefferson, NC,
and London: McFarland & Company, 1990), p. xiv.

77 Excerpt from interview with Bruce Stambler that appears later in this
book. The interview took place at 'Soundstorm', Los Angeles in July
1998. Bruce Stambler has been nominated for five Academy Awards
and has won one for *The Ghost and the Darkness* (1996).

78 Michel Chion's book *The Voice in the Cinema* (New York: Columbia University Press, 1998) deals with this issue in depth.
79 Gary Rydstrom in LoBrutto 1994, p. 245.
80 Scott Chernoff, 'Interview with John Williams', *Star Wars – The Official Magazine* (Issue 21, July/August 1999), pp. 24–28.
81 Needless to say, what exactly the term 'romantic' means to each listener can vary considerably.
82 Animation sound is the one noticeable exception to this rule. This is true especially about the work carried out at Disney and Warner Brothers by legendary figures such as Mel Blanc.
83 This has consequences also in the way film music audiences are regarded as 'less sophisticated' than the more cultured audiences of opera and classical music
84 Jon Burlingate and Gary Crowous, 'Music at the Service of Cinema – An Interview with Ennio Morricone', *Cinéaste* (Vol. 21, Issue 1–2, 1995) – supplement 'Sound and Music in the Movies', p. 80.
85 Claudia Gorbman, 'The State of Film Music Criticism', *Cinéaste* (Vol. 21, Issue 1–2, 1995) – supplement 'Sound and Music in the Movies', p. 74.

4

Interviews with the creators of Dolby: Ioan Allen

It would be difficult to overestimate the importance of Ioan Allen in the development and success of the Dolby Stereo programme. As Ray Dolby suggests earlier in this book, Allen was responsible from the late 1960s onwards for talking to the industry people, filmmakers and exhibitors in an attempt to raise awareness and interest in the newly developed system. In this sense, it is safe to say that more than any other player in the Dolby era Allen has been at the epicentre of change and a passionate voice for Dolby. For his contribution to the development of sound in Hollywood he has been awarded a host of prestigious awards, including an Oscar in 1989, and three Scientific and Engineering Awards from the Academy of Motion Picture Arts and Sciences.

Gianluca Sergi: An easy one to begin with. How did you get into sound?

Ioan Allen: [chuckle] That's not so easy, actually. I left the Navy back in ... a million years ago, then on leaving the Navy I did some technical writing, and oddly enough even though I had left the Navy finished up doing technical writing for admiralty manuals. Then I went through my beatnik phase dressed in black and doing poetry. Then I got into folk music and recording folk music, and that was the introduction into audio. Even though I guess I'd always had an interest in sound in one form or another. I got into rock and roll management, folk music management and recording in general and finally took on a job with Dolby for a temporary job for six months, and I have been there for 33 years now [chuckle].

Sergi: It's been a long temporary job! Ray Dolby said that you actually answered an ad in a newspaper.

Allen: Yeah. Well, it was for a magazine, actually. I don't know how many people applied for the job, but unlike most people I had actually had contact with Dolby noise reduction before when it was still very new. I had been in New York City when the Doors were mixing *Strange Days*, I think it was the *Strange Days* album, and here was this rack of strange grey boxes, and so I got some familiarisation with the equipment, so when I applied for the job with Ray, I was able to say 'yes' I had seen those things before, which was a mind-blower because they were pretty rare on the market at the time.

Sergi: It's interesting that you mention music, and of course everybody knows that Dolby's noise reduction was first used in the music business. The general understanding outside Dolby would be that that was the first market, that's what Ray wanted to go into, and then as an after thought [Dolby] went into movies, but when I talked to Ray he said 'no, no, I always wanted to go into movies'.

Allen: I think he did. He'd had a flurry with the film industry before I joined the company but it was kind of ill thought-out; he thought he could plug in boxes and everything would come out fine, and it didn't. Well, to give you a bit more of the history, when I joined the company, they were selling a few A301 units, the first noise reduction units, mainly for classical recording, but I was able to open the door to rock music recording, and this was simultaneous with the introduction, increasing introduction, of 8- and 16-track tape recorders, but with a degree of luck we stumbled back to victory and did very well with that market place. So that by, I guess, 1972 the market was almost saturated, we had every track of every tape machine, 16-track tape machine, in London, New York, Los Angeles, all equipped with noise reduction, and I started thinking about where else there would be a good market for noise reduction. The only other area where you have literally hundreds of tracks, all of which have a noise build-up was obviously mag [magnetic] recording during pre-mixing in film. I didn't originally think in terms of release prints at all. It was originally just 'let's get these into post-production' and that opened up a whole can of worms because gradually we realised there was a lot more to it than that. One of the triggers was that through classical connections I knew Wendy Carlos in New York, who was famous for *Switched-On Bach*, which I think is still the single biggest-selling classical record of all times, believe it or not.[1] She got hired by Stanley Kubrick to work on *A Clockwork Orange* and this got me an entrée to meet Kubrick at Elstree studios, until finally it was decided that we would use noise reduction on all the pre-mixes of *Clockwork*, which was a real jumping in at the deep end. Also some noise reduction had been used for film recording prior to that, but *Clockwork* was the first movie to use a lot of noise reduction on all the pre-mixes.

Sergi: Was Kubrick particularly excited about using noise reduction?

Allen: Yes. It's a strange relationship between him and sound. He was always very frightened of taking on stereo, partly because of a bad experience on *2001* [*2001: A Space Odyssey*], which is the only film that he actually ever did in stereo, and he wasn't totally comfortable with it because he let it out of his grip and I think he felt deep down that it was a huge thing to learn how to use stereo, but he was happy about the technology of noise reduction for instance, because that didn't affect the way he made the movie, it just made it sound better. He didn't have to suddenly learn how to handle spatial relationships; he could carry on doing the way he had always done it. So he was not a difficult sell to get him to use the noise reduction.

Sergi: Ray [Dolby] says that you were the person who went out to talk to the industry to find out exactly what was needed basically.

Allen: Yeah.

Sergi: Where did you make first contact?

Allen: I went to the studios, and obviously, even though I had travelled in the States a lot because of music recording, I didn't initially do anything in Hollywood. Pinewood and Elstree were the two main contact points, and they were both fairly generous in letting us do tests.² I did a test on a couple of reels of *Jane Eyre*, which I think was done at Pinewood, it was the George C. Scott *Jane Eyre*, experimenting with the use of noise reduction on the release print, because just the use of noise reduction on the pre-mixes didn't seem to do that good; you know, things still sounded pretty bad, so I did an in-out simple version of *Jane Eyre* which is still monitored over what is called the Academy Characteristic. The Academy Curve³ was like a steep roll-off; it's a combination of the loudspeaker, the screen, and even electrical roll off intentionally to reduce the noise. You know, if you turn down the treble control the hiss goes away, but so does the high frequencies. So to compensate the mixer would turn up the highs on the mix. The net result is not only a limited bandwidth but also gross distortion. So in my naivety, all I did in the test of *Jane Eyre* was just to try using noise reduction but leave everything else the way it was, and you would really have to strain to hear a significant difference. There was a little improvement in optical noise but it was still distorted as hell and still had a limited bandwidth, whereupon I realised that to do any good in terms of the perceived quality in the theatre you have to approach these real fundamentals, not only the technology but how people handle it. That led to a couple of years of experiments that I went through changing the B-chain characteristic, throwing out the Academy Curve, determining the optimum curve for the theatre seeing what changes had to follow up in other areas, like the mixers [chuckle]. The mixers would be used always historically to cranking a certain amount of high frequencies up and to teach them not to do that was not an easy task. Also you had to change the choice of microphones because mikes were being picked, selected, that sounded good over this appalling roll-off, you know, so you had to use different microphones. So it's not only the technology, but the techniques had to be changed, and that was a long process. Then we did more demos, like I did a chunk of little re-mixes of *Henry VIII and His Six Wives*, and that started sounding much better. I have always believed that you should be able to get the voice to sound real; it's the most exciting thing in a movie: for anything you do about the surrounds, all that stuff about spatial recording, the most exciting thing is to have this presence in the voice so you are looking at the screen and it's a real experience, this voice is right there with you, and occasionally you get that match. Even today it's rare to do it, to get that quality. I did manage to capture that a couple of times on *Henry VIII* tests, so I had something reasonable to demonstrate. Then I had material I could really start showing around to other studios.

Sergi: What was their reaction?

Allen: Hollywood was the most reluctant to even consider it, there is a certain … [pause] Hollywood likes some things that are invented in Hollywood, but also there is a huge inertia to change within Hollywood, so that was pretty tough going. Then I realised that to make any progress it was the directors you would have to go for. You'd have to look for an imaginative director. Even though Elstree was very supportive, and Pinewood moderately so, they weren't going to go out and get me movies – it had to be at one end the director, and at the other end, the distribution. I realised that we were not geared up to sell direct to theatre chains, so for a short time we had the Rank organisation acting as distributors, which got me another demo film.

Sergi: You've mentioned the Academy Curve, which obviously imposed severe limitations to what could actually be done. I think you referred to it at some point as not sounding much better than a telephone.

Allen: I used to do this little handout sheet, which shows the gradual degradation of frequency response until finally it comes out to about 150 Hz to 3 kHz on an Academy mono track, which is what the audience will hear. You know, at any one point you measure the track it isn't that bad, but if you add all these little bits together that's what you finally finish up with.

Sergi: So would you say that the 'X-curve' was a happy by-product of what you did, or was that the aim?[4]

Allen: Yes. I decided to approach the whole thing from scratch. I must say I give lots of credit to Bill Rover, the mixer at Elstree, and Tony Lumkin, who was chief of sound there, for allowing me to do a lot of stuff that they thought was very strange at the time. I did one test with two BBC loudspeaker monitors, Tannoys, set up very close to the console, so you are very much in the direct field. Then

behind the screen, back there, there were regular cinema Vitavoxes and we played flat recorded speech over the close loudspeakers to get used to them, we then listened to them on the far speakers and then equalised the far speakers until it sounded as close as you could get to being a match. It's never perfectly the same because there are reverberations, to use a different characteristic, but the X-curve as you now know is somewhat close to that.

What people don't realise, and it's been a constant source of frustration to me, is that the X-curve is not a fixed curve, it varies depending on the room size and the reverberation. The idea is that if you have a flat piece of music, or a flat piece of voice, you can play it over the X-curve and it will sound just the same, you won't need to re-equalise it. Unfortunately many theatres, and mix rooms even, are set up as if the X-curve is a fixed feast and it's not. It should really be adjusted to room size, but it started out from being how, in a medium-sized theatre in the early seventies, it would be the correct curve.

I should jump sideways here and tell you something else, which vaguely introduces the concept of spatial sound, which is that 99 per cent of the movies in the early seventies, the period we're are talking about, were just recorded in mono, and released in mono optical, but there are a few that were being realised in 4-track mag stripe, and the mag stripe characteristic is not a full Academy Curve. It's half way, if you like, between the Academy Curve and the X-curve and it was the characteristic you would get if you just had a raw loudspeaker behind the screen with a fairly bad loud-speaker and a fairly bad screen, but without the extra filters that are put in the Academy Curve. So a lot of the film industry would say that's good enough, and that curve, which is now obsolete, was tentatively called the 'N-curve', as I remember, the normal curve, 'N' stood for, whilst 'X' stood for experimental. So there were films with that middle characteristic which still suffered from pre-emphasis distortion that you get on the mag stripe and a lot of technical problems with mag striping.

Sergi: And I presume they were very expensive.

Allen: Unbelievably, because you have to record in real time. I used to joke in lectures, I used to talk about somebody with the bucket, bucket and brush, painting the stripe down. But you have to make the film print the picture, then stripe it, then you have to wait 48 hours for it to dry, theoretically, then you have to record on it in real time, so obviously the cost is huge, compared to the cost of a photographical optical.

Sergi: By that stage obviously there weren't many cinemas equipped to play magnetic stereo anyway?

Allen: A dwindling number, they were closing all the time and they were not maintaining the stripe equipment: the penthouse is expensive, it's difficult to thread for the projectionist, the heads would wear out. Theoretically the heads had to be changed once a month: if you were running 70 mm and at 2,000 dollars a month, say 1,000 pounds a month for the sake of argument, nobody is going to do that, so as a result the heads would totally wear out. If you think about a cassette tape, it's really soft and it wraps around the head, but if you think about film, it's very stiff and in order to get the high-frequency contact it really has to pull hard against the head and it becomes like putty and just wears away, and then the highs disappear.

Sergi: Were you at this stage already thinking about stereo? The information on the Dolby history from Dolby's own web site says something about 'false start'. In other words, the improvements that you brought in with the Dolby noise reduction system were on monophonic soundtracks, and that was not enough, as it were, to change, the industry.

Allen: We did four or five movies in Dolby mono, probably one of the most famous ones was the *Rocky Horror Picture Show*, which in the States was actually released in conventional optical but it was released in Dolby mono in England. And yes, there was slow penetration, unbelievably slow. Ron Uhlig at Eastman Kodak was playing with 16 mm at splitting the track in two. The track had been split in two before – this was not really a revolutionary concept – John Frayne had done this in 1953. Youlig did the same thing and used Dolby B-type noise reduction to reduce the hiss on 16 mm because Kodak wanted to compete with the U-Matic market and said 'we've got stereo too'.[5] Nobody ever used it but he demonstrated it. I got to know him, and I thought 'well, we can do something with stereo on 35 mm' because I have always been a stereo fan when mono was the norm and I became a quad fan when stereo was the norm.

I think it's safe to say that Ray and I didn't really agree, he was not a format king. He really believed in selling noise reduction and I was saying not only should we be getting into a format but we need to build unique units for the theatre market which at first he was reluctant to concede to, for quite sensible reasons: a small company does not want to dilute with too wide a product line. But I said 'this is the only way we can get this to fly, with dedicated units and a format'. In 1974 we took over the 16 mm stereo camera from Eastman Kodak, which is actually owned by RCA, and shipped it to Elstree in England, converted it to 35 mm and I did some demo pieces. Then we did a demo reel from *Stardust*, Michael Apted movie, which I still have and use it for demonstration purposes in the history lectures. Apart from the fact that we got left and right flipped, it plays just fine today [chuckle]. No surround obviously, it was just stereo. We took it to the SMPTE conference in Toronto in November 1974.

And lo and behold there's at least one other stereo system being suggested for stereo optical! The most interesting one was a guy called Petra Ulahos who at the time was in full-time employment with the Motion Picture Research Council organisation, which is a Hollywood home bred and who would pay for these developments to be done in Hollywood. Petra Ulahos' system used colour to modulate three tree tracks and had this kind of push–pull arrangement. It did kind of work, but if you know how film fades you know how getting the balance right in an individual track was probably problematical in the long run and it looked very expensive to convert the projectors and of course it was totally incompatible: you couldn't play it on an unconverted projector. Well, we went in and demonstrated our reel of *Stardust*. It was stereo and it was a regular black and white photographic print and we had a nice centre channel. Here's a little technical aside for you: its always a better idea to have to code more channels into fewer tracks if you can get the separation you need, the reason being that the tracks become more stable, you get a better signal-to-noise ratio, less affected by dirt, so it's always better to code three into two than it would be to have three separate tracks, and that becomes even more true when you get to four tracks and four channels. So our demonstration was a real hit, and because you could play the demo on an unconverted projector, it would cost zero to do it, and it's stereo. That was not the end of the story by any means but in terms of getting the technical community to sit up and pay notice that was a pretty big impact.

Sergi: So would you say the first step was to go from mono to three channels, in other words to get there step by step, not jump?

Allen: Yes, yes. Then we did a few movies in three channels, and to get things really started that was when I really started to realise you had to go to the film directors, you had to get imaginative directors on your side. The first director to like the idea was Ken Russell and we did *Lisztomania*, which was not greeted with a great box office success but was a good learning curve for me. I forget how many films we did, maybe half a dozen films that were stereo without surround. Then I wanted to get the big musical in 1976, which was *A Star is Born*, Barbra Streisand film, out in stereo optical. We had a couple of meetings with her in Hollywood. She would only do it, or her people would only do it, if there was a surround channel on it, because they thought the surround and crowd noise were really important. So I went to the engineering department at Dolby and said 'could we do this, could we do surrounds?' 'Oh yeah, no problem!'. This is about July and the release is in December. Come October I realise we are in deep doo doo! [laughter]. By that time I was a 4-channel fan and was really into matrixes at home, so I kluged, for wanted of a better word, I 'kluged' together a matrix system to be able to say to the Streisand folk, 'yes, here we are, we've got a 4-channel system'. I think we equipped six theatres and they were able to say 'we have done it'.

Sergi: Do you remember where they were?

Allen: No. New York, Los Angeles I expect. The film was also released in 4-track mag conventional, nothing to do with Dolby, and 6-track mag on the 70 mm. The 70 mm thing is really interesting, because at the time the way the 70 mm mixes were made was to do with what was called a 'spread', which is: you take left centre and right from the 4-track mix and literally combine left and centre to create half-left, and centre and right to create half-right. Seeing that there wasn't much separation in the music recording in the first place what finished up is a gorgeous big out-of-phase mono which really sounded unpleasant to me, though it was nothing unique to *A Star is Born*, that was the way all the films were being done at that time I think. So I thought what a waste this is, this is just down-turn.

At the time Steve Katz, who was our guy in Hollywood, met Gary Kurtz who was the producer of *Star Wars* and arranged for me to meet with Gary. He wanted obviously to have 70 mm capability on *Star Wars*, and I thought 'there has to be some better way of doing this'. I said 'let's do it a different way: let's throw out 2 and 4 as prime channels and use those to carry low frequencies'. I had to convince people this would work, so we did a demo at the Academy Theatre for Gary Kurtz and a couple of other people, I cannot remember who was there now. We took a section from *Capricorn One* and remixed it two ways: one, which came to be known as 'Baby Boom', which is used as bass extension, and one just doing the taper. Gary Kurtz obviously picked what we were doing for the low-frequency extension, so *Star Wars* in 1977 was the first film with low-frequency extension on it, which worked pretty well and that became the pattern for 70 mm films for years to come.

Gary was unique in that he really cared about the sound a lot. I think he triggered George Lucas's interest in sound, I think it came initially from him. When it was decided that they would do a Dolby stereo release on *Star Wars*, uniquely he said he would meet us before this film starts because sound was not going to be the after-thought. So he set up a lunch with Derek Ball, the sound recordist, and George and he and I, at the Grosvenor Hotel, I think it was, in Elstree and literally said 'what do you want us to do in terms of how the sound should be recorded?' At the time there was an increasing use of Lavelier microphones but I said 'no, no, no, I want wherever possible the boom mikes, boom mikes, boom mikes'. Derek actually used to boom on a lot of the recording in *Star Wars* with great results. There is one of my magic lines in *Star Wars* when Alec Guinness says 'before the dark times, before the empire' and this is electric, when you hear that in the theatre to this day. Even though it's Dolby A-type, a fairly old technology, it still springs to life: this guy is in the room with you, and that's because [he was recorded] using a boom mike. The mike is seeing the lips, it's probably 3 feet away, just an exquisite recording. That kind of facility was triggered by Gary Kurtz to allow us to get to talk to the sound recordist beforehand, to say 'this is how we think it should be done'.

Sergi: That confirms what I have heard from other people, that although there had been other films before it, *Star Wars* was really the film where sound was taken much more into account from the very beginning, and where you were involved from the beginning.

Allen: Yeah.

Sergi: Was that the first time Dolby technicians helping on set came to be known and credited as 'Dolby consultants'?

Allen: No, we had had that before in that because the technology was fairly new, there had been a Dolby consultant since the first mono film. It got formalised after *Star Wars*, and we started getting credits.

Sergi: Steve Katz was credited as the Dolby consultant on *Star Wars*.

Allen: Yeah, both he and I spent a lot of time on *Star Wars* [chuckle]. And you know, Fox didn't realise what they had, there was a lot of problems in getting their cooperation in what seemed to them like a revolutionary technology: who needs it? And they weren't sure the movie was that hot a movie.

Sergi: Had you been speaking to exhibitors at this point saying 'look, this new system is going to come out' or did you leave it to the studio?

Allen: Yes. Once Fox knew they had a real hit on their hands they were pretty helpful in talking to the theatres to persuade them to put in Dolby units, because the pattern of releases in those days was not like today with 5,000 prints on a Friday and the movie is over the following week. There was a slower roll-out. There was a fair amount of cooperation, but also we started working theatre trade shows like Show West and the NATO Show. The year after

Star Wars this guy, a theatre owner, came up to me at a trade show and said 'thanks very much for the Cadillac', and I said 'what do you mean Cadillac?' and he said 'well, I came to see you last year and I said 1) should I book *Star Wars* and 2) should I put it in a Dolby unit and you said yes on both counts and it's paid for the Cadillac. It's outside right now, thanks very much.' [Laugh]

Sergi: Were you directly involved in the post-production process of *Star Wars*?

Allen: Yeah, Steve probably spent more time than I did, but, as usual, it was a post-production nightmare of pre-mixing at night and mixing during the day. We had a sofa in the dubbing theatre to sleep on and stuff like that.

Sergi: Did *Star Wars* help you increase sales?

Allen: Yes, *Star Wars* accelerated things. We were making progress before *Star Wars* and I couldn't be sure, but I would guess there were 50 theatres equipped by the time we had finished the *Star is Born* which was December of 1976, but there was no doubt that *Star Wars* was a significant help. But that instantly led into some other films that we got at the end of 1977, like *Close Encounters*. The problem we had, if there was a problem, was that we got associated with that kind of film, so science fiction, loud, lots of stereo surround effects, that's what Dolby meant. It wasn't until probably *Days of Heaven*, Terry Malick's film, that I managed to get across this idea that every film can benefit [from using Dolby], that quiet, low-level stereo ambiences do as much to help a film as loud spatial sound effects. That's been an ongoing battle to this day. You know, people don't realise what can be done with low-level sound effects in terms of putting the audience into the environment that it sees on the screen. Some directors will say 'well, there's not much value for surrounds in my movie' just because there are not flyovers, you know. Well, flyovers is the vulgar extreme, and the real meat and potatoes of surrounds I believe is ambiences, the field of waving corn is wonderful at putting you in the action.

Sergi: You mentioned earlier the role of Dolby consultants; could you explain more about their role and the impact of their contribution?

Allen: Back in the mid-1970s even Dolby mono represented significant technological change in the mix room. Not only was radically new equipment required, with new alignment procedures, but also the mix process itself was radically changed. Moving from the Academy Characteristic to the X-curve meant that everything 'sounded different'. Mixers were used to certain types of microphone, and typical equalisation changes needed to make things 'sound right'. Now they were being asked to listen anew, and re-evaluate techniques they had used since time immemorial. Changes meant more than just adjusting the treble control for the obvious difference between the Academy [curve] and the X-curve. The X-curve was much closer to flat at low frequencies, and this meant that a voice could sound more real, but also resulted in low-frequency extraneous noise becoming more apparent – traffic, generator noise etc. New techniques and equipment were required to remove these noise blankets, which were previously inaudible. Another change, and perhaps one of our major industry contributions, was the establishment of a calibrated monitor level – ensuring the possibility that every mix room had monitor/loudspeaker systems set at the same level, and that theatres were set to the same level for audience playback.

Together this was all so much, that a Dolby consultant became pretty much a resident engineer during the early films. I certainly spent many days in the UK dubbing theatres in the mid-seventies, and Steve Katz worked full-time on the early movies in Hollywood. Technological change was further introduced with the stereo optical track [matrix technology] and improved methods for and calibration of 70 mm magnetic.

It soon became apparent that some directors expected more from the Dolby consultant than a guy with a screwdriver aligning equipment. In some cases the Dolby engineer would be asked to sit with the director, and give advice on how to use the new technology to best advantage. And he would also have to carefully walk the 'electro-political tightrope', effecting change without upsetting the players. It was not unusual for a Dolby consultant to be 'thrown off the lot' after drawing attention to a technical problem which others would rather sweep under the carpet! Invariably, though, he would be allowed back on to the stage when tempers cooled. Indeed, the phrase 'electro-political tightrope' was coined by Bill Mead, one of the early Dolby consultants.

By the late 1970s, I realised that different strokes applied to different folks. All mixes had a substantial Dolby presence, from beginning to end of the mix. But some mixers wanted more active artistic input from the Dolby-guy – while others expected him to sit quietly and just fix any technical problems that came along. So, as we hired more Dolby engineers, where possible we would select an engineer to suit a specific show's needs. And we would try to keep one single person as the engineer attached to a show all the way through, from pre-production planning [rare], to mix, checking answer prints and laboratory printing, attending previews, and even general theatre checks in selected key houses for commercial release.

By the early eighties things had changed. There were far too many movies for us to be able to provide personnel for this kind of exhaustive support, and fortuitously mixers were getting used to the new technology. So we established a minimum subset of Dolby attendance – what we needed to ensure the mix met technical standards to justify use of the Dolby trademark. This minimum set included checking mix-room characteristics prior to the first day of the mix – checking room tuning, levels, equipment calibration. Then attendance during the final mix, ensuring that there were no overloads or unforeseen technical problems. This minimum subset exists to this day, so every mix is still checked for acceptable technical conformance. Of course, some directors and mixers will still ask for much more contribution from the Dolby consultant – but today it would be very rare for him to attend every minute of the mix.

Sergi: Two aspects have been highlighted by many people as being particularly significant to the success of Dolby stereo systems. First of all it was compatible with existing stereo systems?

Allen: Yes. Existing mono systems. We have always fought for that: every format that I have been involved with, you'd be able to play with your existing equipment. Historically the theatre industry buys a 35mm projector, they expect thirty or forty years of life from it, and it will work for fifty years probably. Even though they will buy themselves a new car every spring, the equipment in the booth is expected to go on forever. So I have always believed in making it possible for that theatre to go on for a long time, not fifty years God help us! [chuckle] But a long time, and by and large when they realise they are not being forced into it, they are much more cooperative. The studios historically have done some pretty mean things for the theatres ... that's unfair, *some* studios have done some pretty mean things: they have come out with a format that is only destined for one movie, persuade the theatres really hard to buy something that becomes obsolescent instantly because they have played that film, so I have always said 'well you will never be obsolescent'. Dolby stereo before surround was compatible with mono, surround was compatible with stereo or mono, A-type was superseded by SR but you can play back even an A-type track on an SR playback and vice versa. Actually that's not true: you can play back SR on an A-type playback but not the other way round. In every case the theatre owner has not been forced to update even when we got to digital: the theatre owner has not been forced to buy the digital adapter because he can still playback the SR track and I think that's what's given us a lot of credibility, by not trying to squeeze the theatre owners and forcing them to buy something. Market pressures may persuade them strongly to buy something, because they want to compete with the guy down the road, but they have always had the ability to playback.

Sergi: The other key factor would appear to be cost, especially if compared to previous systems like magnetic sound.

Allen: Yes. Well, that's cheaper at both ends of the scale: it's much cheaper for print production because it's all photographic, and in terms of theatre maintenance costs it's zero once you've got it.

Sergi: Would you agree that cost and backward compatibility are cardinal points in the success of the programme, other than quality obviously?

Allen: Yeah. Our equipment in the booth costs a lot less than the complete set of loud speakers that you need today, or a comparable amount, but it's certainly not the dominant factor in new equipment costs.

Sergi: Somewhere in the literature of Dolby there is an interesting claim that one of the reasons why Dolby has been so successful has been because it has not been tied to any specific studio and has maintained an 'aura' of independence about it.

Allen: Yeah, in the soundtrack formats, or even picture formats, that come from different studios which have limited widespread appeal because this belongs to Fox, or that belongs to Universal or that belongs to whatever. But on the other side, because we are not Hollywood based, that's the downside, it was difficult to get going, you know. Nowadays of course we are thought of as being a Hollywood company because we have offices there, people there, but in the seventies and early eighties we were definitely thought of as very weird from out of town.

Sergi: And also of course now, as an aside, San Francisco is widely recognised as the epicentre of film sound.

Allen: But you know Hollywood really resents San Francisco; they don't like films going off there to do post [post-production], it's very much 'those other guys'. And Hollywood used to resent people going to post in England.

Sergi: I was going to ask you about that actually.

Allen: It's the same thing, I think. And also of course, Northern California has been remarkably successful in picking up Oscars.

Sergi: Yes, indeed. Now I was going to ask you ...

Allen: And is there a different style of mixing, you are going to ask me.

Sergi: That's exactly one of the things I wanted to talk about [chuckle], yeah.

Allen: [laugh].

Sergi: I've asked several sound designers about it because you can, at times, tell apart films that have been mixed in New York from films that have been mixed in Los Angeles from those that have been mixed in San Francisco. Most of those I've spoken to agree but not many people can actually give me a precise idea as to why that's the case. Somebody once told me that New York has much smaller dubbing theatres and therefore, for example, they tend to use less surround because they are much smaller and compact. Whereas San Francisco, at places like Skywalker Sound, they have almost a full-sized theatre where they can dub. My feeling is that the three cities actually sound very different.

Allen: Yes, there's more to it than the room size, I'm sure. You get a local style that comes from the mixers, the directors who are working with those mixers. In New York, for example I think Sydney Lumet is not a great surround fan, so he does a couple of movies there so that the mixer becomes not terribly surround orientated.

Sergi: Or Woody Allen.

Allen: Well, Woody Allen is not stereo orientated.

Sergi: Indeed.

Allen: Yeah, so it becomes a style rather than a room size. I think one effect of the room size may be dynamic range: there is less dynamic range in New York mixes, their range from loud to quiet is a bit narrow. But I think that is cultural, let's use that word. There is a Skywalker culture, comes from Ben Burt, Gary Summers, Gary Rydstrom, a whole tradition. And oddly enough that, of course, is different from the world of Murch's tradition, which is also a Northern Californian tradition. Something else has occurred to me about this, which is the director who says to you 'my story's on the screen I don't need surrounds' and there are different styles of directorial use of the surrounds for that reason. Then you get down to the issue about how the soundtrack is trying to capture what you see on the screen: is it being a faithful representation of the action you see or is it more of a stylised storytelling in its own right? In one of my lectures I talk about the street scene when the hero the protagonist and his girlfriend are walking in a crowd and there's lots of cars and buses passing, and it's obviously manifestly impossible to capture that scene. If you did capture everything it would become a totally strangled mess, even if you could hear what they are saying, so you represent the twelve cars that you can see by one car noise. Pudovkin said that if sound is used simply to represent what you see on the screen you are dead in the water. I'm paraphrasing grossly, what you should be doing is creating sound as a separate montage in its own right. Well, I think you'll find as you go from directors in New York to, well, not necessarily directors but the 'culture' of New York mixing, and the culture of San Francisco mixing and the culture of Los Angeles there are variations on that curve as to whether or not you are trying to capture what you see in its entirety or whether you are doing a stylised difference, you know. There is a scene in *Jurassic Park*, a close-up scene, where a Zippo lighter goes CLICK, and it's so loud, that the audience jump out of their shoes. That's what Walter Murch calls a narrative effect as opposed to an effect effect. In other words, it's not a background, in a sense it's a marker, it's totally unrealistic. Here's a soundtrack which has been developed not on a realistic basis, consciously. I think those different cultures become New York based or Los Angeles based or San Francisco based or London based as well.

Sergi: Yes, that would tally with my personal impression of it, that there is another dimension to San Francisco mixing, and you can almost hear it, partly because of the people who work here, but as you say then eventually it becomes a culture, a tradition.

Allen: I lecture in Norway, every year. I go to the Norwegian Short Film Festival, I run a jury there, evaluating Norwegian short films, some which are over an hour long [laughs]. I lecture at it and at the end do an hour and a half retrospective and go through their films and analyse the sound quality of each. Again and again and again I am having to ram home this idea of 'do a sound story board before you start the movie'. Invariably one or two directors will, but the vast majority won't, because – to use your own phrase – sound has got forgotten until 'oh my God, we have got to do this sound now!' and it's too late. And the person who does the sound story board can work out beforehand where the sound should be realistic, where it should be symbolic, how wide the stereo should be, as almost alongside the script to get an idea, so you finish up with a sound sculpture that is helping the story rather than it just being a kind of 'drag it along with the storyline later on'.

Sergi: However, that I would think depends also on production practices. I mean, as you said, in some cases you get pre-production meetings where sound people are invited so that they can kind of get to know where people want to go with the film, but most of the sound people I've spoken to complain that that's still pretty rare.

Allen: Yes it is.

Sergi: A lot of the times they are called in too late and then it becomes very difficult.

Allen: Randy [Thom] got involved with the first Surround EX film in Japan, *Avalon* a couple of years ago. I suggested Randy Thom and he was called in at pretty much the last minute as sound effects designer, after the film had been completely structured. And even though there are some wonderful sound design in there, it almost reads like an after-thought, because it wasn't part of the original design.

Sergi: Indeed. Some designers, especially people like Randy [Thom] and to a certain extent Gary [Rydstrom], are 'political' in the sense of trying to convince the industry at large to give more attention to sound. Randy for example has written lots of small pamphlets, as it were, on the importance of considering sound early on. Gary was telling me that sound people still get only end credits because the Director's Guild of America considers sound as a technical part of filmmaking.

Allen: No [pause] Well, it may be policy actually, but there has been a complete swing. I mean in 1931/32 the sound director was on a par with the picture director, he would say 'stop it we are going to shoot that again'. Nowadays he would get shot if he tried to do something like that. By the sixties sound was just a kind of throwaway; then Ben Burt was the first person to get credited as a sound designer, and there was a kind of recovery and sound designers started getting credits, albeit below the line; they're not above the line, but they are credits. I think you'll find that Larry Blake I think has had above-the-line credits for Stephen Soderbergh. I always got really upset in the US by the sound mixer having such a lowly credit in the end credits section, but let's face it, the audience doesn't stay and watch the end credits anyway.

Sergi: No, but it is important on a variety of other levels, in terms of signalling the status of sound in many ways. I mean, imagine if the director got a credit like that, he or she would have a fit!

Allen: Yeah. Sound and picture are both trying to tell the story, and then it is ridiculous that the sound mixer should be below the third grip, down in the end credits, you know.

Sergi: Is it true that sound often accounts for about 1 per cent of the overall budget whereas special visual effects costs run into tens of millions of dollars?

Allen: It's very difficult to do those sums, you know, about percentages. That's probably right, but it's very difficult to say what the budget is. It's really the concentration that's required, not the actual money. In other words, the pre-production meeting showing that they really care about the sound is not expensive, but it's worth its weight in gold.

Sergi: Indeed, but because it costs so little some people will consider it as being less important because it's not a huge problem if you don't do a good job, whereas if you mess up a hundred million dollars' worth of visual effects then you're dead.

Allen: Yes, that's true. One of the things I do with film students is talk about what can go wrong during the course of the mix. I break it into three sections, what can go wrong on location recording, in post and in the theatre, and see how many things they can come up with as students. In post the one thing they never come up with is what I claim is 'the accountant': the accountant sees the rough cut and says 'fine, release it' – 'but we haven't done the sound yet' – 'well, it sounded OK to me, you know, release it' [chuckle]. There is no doubt, and Gary would certainly support this, that the time available for post sound has been greatly truncated in the last fifteen to twenty years. It's now half of what it was twenty years ago, and you can hear that in some of the mixes.

Sergi: Ok, I'd like to take you back for a moment to the development at Dolby. You mention in an article that digital sound was 'the next logical step' after Dolby became established. I can see the music industry was already going in that direction, but why was it logical?

Allen: Well, for marketing reasons. There was CDS, you know, which is the original digital system which hit the market.[6] But that was a flawed system because they made the fundamental mistake of putting the digital data in the analogue area so they had no fall-back, and you couldn't move it from screen to screen, you couldn't down dump the print, that was just a real bad engineering concept. But it worked with some difficulty, the bits were too small, but it was apparently to us that you had to be ready to compete with a digital system. Also to be honest with you, the public was extremely gullible and believed that digital would sound better, digital was the magic word you know, pretty soon we'll have digital toenail clippers, they are going to be really wonderful. So, for actually about ten years before we released the digital system we'd had this background engineering programme working on different ways to do it and looking at different areas of the film, believe it or not we even thought about putting holograms in the picture area and stuff like this, but all of them were predicated on the one idea which was to retain compatibility, so that the SR track would stay in the analogue area, we're not going to fuss with that and put it somewhere else. I'll give you a little technical aside which may be of interest. Why did we settle on the area between the sprockets? People didn't realise we actually did a lot of research on that and we put black film between trailers and features on shows that ran in New York, Chicago and various cities across the country and then let them play for a certain number of plays, 100 plays, 200 plays, 500 plays in one case, pull all the black film back to look to see where all the scratches were, how much dirt there was, where the dirt was worse and, believe it or not, what shape the dirt was and which direction the dirt was lying in. That's a key issue in determining the bit size, whether the bit should be square or rectangular, and if it's rectangular what direction it should be in, until we finally decided on square and then decided that the area between the sprocket was the best thing to do. The original idea I had was to put it in the frameline between picture frames because when the film comes down and stops it's a beautiful time to scan it and that would have been just really neat, tons of area, works fine on 1:1:85 but unfortunately on scope you'd have to change the picture format and the prospect of changing picture format in every theatre I just thought was 'oh, am I going to take that on, life's tough enough' so we then went into the sprocket area, announced it, and really I don't think we knew how well it would take it on, I didn't know how many theatres we're going to take it on because we'd had what to our ears was a really superb-sounding analogue sounding SR and what digital had to offer was greater dynamic range, definitely and the ability to do stereo surrounds. What's interesting is that on 70 mm we had had stereo surrounds since *Superman* in 1978 and it was very rarely used by 70 mm mixes, but for some reason when digital was available on the optical, everyone wants stereo surround, even though to this day there is a paucity of real stuff on those that really use stereo surrounds. There's a lot of mono panning of stuff you know, but in terms of 4-channel ambiences nobody is doing that, very few people are, and yet it brings the theatre to life with a real 4-channel ambience.

Sergi: Indeed. OK, now this is a very interesting time, because for the first time you get real competition from other digital systems. Did that change in any way your approach do you think? One question for example is particularly interesting to ask: why didn't you get more competition before, why does it happen now?

Allen: There's always been competition; this is a misunderstanding. There were films being mixed by Ultra Stereo. To be honest with you, in theatres, I wouldn't want 100 per cent of the market anyway; you'd be really resented if you were the only choice. I'm not sure what the magic number is but to lose 25 per cent or 30 per cent of the market, I think that's just fine so that people have a free choice and I'd like them to come to us because (we have) the best box, the best price, the most reliable, the best support the best service and the best sound, but I'd like them to have a choice of something worse for them to compare it with.

Sergi: I have one question about the future. When Tom Bruchs was showing me around in the back of your demo theatre at Dolby Labs he said that you are going to actually discretely amplify each of the 17 speakers of the surround array to do some tests.[7] Now that would kind of suggest that that's the next step forward, to try and have more channels there. Some people have experimented with overhead channels, as in the case of *We Were Soldiers*. Is that where we are going next?

Allen: Well, I have a real prejudice against general use of ceiling speakers, because those of us who were brought up with ceiling speakers in the sixties know how awful they are to maintain, and how difficult it is to get coverage, but I can see that for a film like *We Were Soldiers* it would make some sense, but only for a very minority of films. But then you have to say to yourself, where do I throw my bit space? You throw your bit space at where the most important channels are, and that's behind the screen.

Notes

1   Wendy Carlos had a huge hit in 1968 with *Switched-On Bach*, one of the first recordings to raise awareness about the Moog synthesiser, for which she won three Grammy Awards. Since then, she worked with Stanley Kubrick on *A Clockwork Orange*, and *The Shining*, as well as composing the music score for Disney's *Tron* in 1982.

2   Pinewood Studios and Elstree Studios are both located near London.

3   The Academy Characteristic is often referred to as the 'Academy Curve'.

4   The 'X-curve' replaced the 'Academy Curve' as the industry standard and was directly inspired by the improvements brought about by the development of Dolby's technologies.

5   U-Matic was a ¾-inch videotape system created by Sony in the late 1960s.

6   CDS (Cinema Digital Sound) was pioneered with the 70 mm release of several films in 1990/1991, including *Dick Tracy*, *Edward Scissorhands*, *Terminator 2: Judgment Day* and *Days of Thunder*.

7   Tom Bruchs is the engineer in charge of Dolby's projection booth technology and of the film theatre at Dolby's Headquarters in San Francisco that is used for tests and demonstrations.

Part II

Listening to movies

Introduction: bridging the gap

In this section my main aim is to bridge the gap between a general understanding that sound matters to actually considering sound as an integral part of analysis and research. In particular, I will look at the ways in which sound practitioners think about sound, organise their material, and how scholars can attempt to understand how sound works in contemporary cinema.

One of the most defining features of the Dolby era has been the development of professional figures old and new. In the pre-Dolby era, sound credits were conventionally attributed to a single figure, usually a 'sound engineer'. This was customarily the head of the sound department within any given studio. In other words, if audiences and critics were to judge from credits alone, it would appear that a handful of people were enough to put together even the most complicated of soundtracks, whilst reinforcing the notion of sound people as technicians (in this sense, the word 'engineer' is a strong indication of attitudes to sound within the industry). The arrival of the new generation of sound men and women whose work in the 1970s was crucial in establishing Dolby as a creative and techno-logical force has since then challenged established patterns of pro-duction as well as existing views on the nature of sound work. As I have indicated earlier, the sound-conscious generation of film-makers that had spawned Lucas, Spielberg, Scorsese and Coppola identified early on in their careers the importance of considering sound as a key element rather than just an add-on. Importantly, this new rank of film sound practitioners had attended film schools just as, and sometimes with, those same directors who were now begin-ning to impose themselves as the new leading group in Hollywood cinema. Lucas hired Burtt for *Star Wars* almost immediately after

Burtt had finished film school at USC, the same university Lucas himself had attended.[1] Murch was also a USC film-school graduate and, indeed, a college mate of Lucas. The director with whom he would become most commonly associated with, Francis Ford Coppola, had also attended film school, but across town at UCLA.[2] Indeed, film schools such as USC and UCLA, both in Los Angeles, and NYU in New York have since provided a steady flow of creative talent. This new breed of film professionals had been exposed to notions of auteurism in their studies and understood well the political and cultural implications that arose from those established views on creative responsibility. It is therefore unsurprising that the work of this new pool of sound talent should show the signs of an impressive sense of confidence in the creative potential of sound coupled with a similarly remarkable will to claim a more substantial role in the filmmaking hierarchy. The latter point is of particular importance to the development of sound aesthetics in the Dolby era for it would be difficult to imagine soundtracks as innovative as those of *Star Wars*, *Apocalypse Now*, *The Right Stuff* and *Raiders of the Lost Ark* without the privileged position that sound people working on those films enjoyed in terms of time allowed, relationship with the director, and early involvement in the filmmaking process. In this sense, the 'political' involvement of key people such as Murch, Thom and Rydstrom, amongst others, in raising awareness of the creative contribution that sound people bring to a movie is illuminating.

The widely documented move by Coppola and Murch to credit the latter with 'Sound Montage' and 'Sound Design' credits represented the first real attempt at addressing the central issue of the 'status' of film sound and thus of sound people.[3] In particular, the main concern seems to have been that of challenging the view, commonly held both in filmmaking and academic circles, that sound is merely a 'technical issue' and, by extension, that sound people are 'technicians'. Since then, the most successful designers have attained the kind of status that pre-Dolby generations of sound people neither dreamed of nor dared to pursue. The issue of status is central to the creative effort because there would appear to be a clear correlation between the status of a sound person and the level of his or her engagement in the decision-making process: the higher the status, the earlier the involvement. Because many sound people have highlighted the importance of getting involved as early as possible in a film project so as to be able to have a say in decisions that might later impact on the soundtrack, the issue of status and level of engagement in the filmmaking process are part of the same argument.[4]

There are two main reasons for choosing Gary Rydstrom and Bruce Stambler over other interviewees that I could have included here. First, their work and expertise cover a wide spectrum within film sound production. Rydstrom talks eloquently about the two roles he has most often been involved with, namely that of Sound Designer and Re-recording Mixer. Bruce Stambler's views are indicative of the kind of thinking that a Supervising Sound Editor follows in creating and organising a soundtrack. Second, they have been very successful in their work. Rydstrom, a winner of seven Oscars, is undoubtedly the most successful designer of his generation and has been a key factor in developing the world's leading post-production facility, Skywalker Sound, as well as being the inspiration behind the development of Dolby's EX sound system. Stambler, himself an Oscar winner, is one of the major contributors within Soundstorm, a leading post-production facility in Hollywood. His views also offer an insight into the politics of sound making and the sometimes awkward position a sound editor can find him- or herself in. Although different in outlook and creative approach, their status and contribution to contemporary film sound marks them as belonging to a cohesive 'elite group', whose views and work have shaped the Dolby era in creative, institutional and technological terms.[5] More specifically, I was impressed by how revealing their thoughts and views were, not simply about the sound-making process but also on the Hollywood filmmaking process as a whole. Both Stambler and Rydstrom offer a rare insight into the mechanics and politics of contemporary filmmaking and as such their views are valuable in ways that exceed the confines of my book. These interviews also proved to be the ideal frame within which to place my attempt at suggesting ways in which scholars could begin to think about the way sound works in a movie and how it contributes to the film as a whole.

Notes

1 USC is the abbreviation with which the University of Southern California in Los Angeles is commonly known. For more information see www.usc.edu (accessed 1 January 2003).

2 UCLA is the abbreviation with which the University of California at
   Los Angeles is commonly known. For more information see
   www.ucla.edu (accessed 1 January 2003).
3 The actual 'birth' of the term Sound Designer owes more to accident
   than design. Coppola and Murch settled on the term Sound Designer
   since Murch was not a union member and could therefore not be credited with one of the traditional sound credits, such as Supervising
   Sound Editor. However, the term Sound Designer quickly became a
   'political' credit with a considerable amount of prestige attached to it.
4 As Gary Rydstrom points out in the interview in Chapter 3, this is an
   ongoing struggle. This is true in particular in relation to the Directors'
   Guild of America's refusal to acknowledge that sound is worthy of
   more than the 'technical' credit status that is given at present. This is
   an important issue, because it pushes sound credits to the tail end of a
   movie's credits as technical credits that are not allowed to be 'head'
   credits on a movie.
5 It is worth pointing out they know each other and have in the past
   exchanged ideas and views about their work.

Interviews with the makers of sound: Bruce Stambler

Bruce Stambler is a supervising sound editor at Soundstorm, a sound facility based in Los Angeles.[1] He has been nominated five times for an Academy Award and won one for *The Ghost and the Darkness*.

He has worked with some of Hollywood's most successful directors, on pictures such as *Under Siege*, *The Fugitive*, *Batman and Robin* and *Clear and Present Danger*. I met Bruce while he was preparing the final mix for *Pleasantville* at Todd-AO West in Radford, Los Angeles.

Gianluca Sergi: Let's start from the beginning. How did you get into film sound?

Bruce Stambler: I started as an apprentice at Universal Studios when I was 26, and I worked in film shipping. Then I worked in features, in editorial, for another year. Then I was offered an opportunity – somebody said 'Do you want to be an assistant sound editor?', I thought, a SOUND editor? That sounds good! [laughs]. I was an assistant for a couple of years at Universal still, I did a lot of TV, six, seven days a week, from six in the morning to ten at night, and then they moved me up to editor and trailers, TV trailers. I didn't screw those up and they moved me to half-hour TV shows, and if you didn't screw those up then they'd give you an hour TV show. Finally someone gave me a job on a feature as sound editor and eventually as a supervisor.

Sergi: Would you say that money is definitely an issue in sound?

Stambler: Yeah, money is a big issue. Money is something that you need to control best you can. Unfortunately, the whole artistic aspect of doing what we do leaves a lot of decisions that affect money. Visually a picture changes, and there is constant editorial. That's what they call it, editorial. And editorials comprise of picture, sound and music; they are not separate, they all work together. That means that everybody is changing their ideas and artistic inputs and when you have that, depending on the complexity of the movie, you can get into huge dollars.

My job is to try to control the artistic part as well as the financial part, I HAVE to, I have to and I always bring it to their attention. It is my responsibility and I always say 'I can spend the money with the best of them, but I can help you control and save some money too if you are willing to sit down and talk about these issues and things that we can work together on to control the budget'. This is how you get a movie. I have a set of clients that I work with, and the director or producer will call me and say 'Stambler, I want you to do my movie', whatever it is, then you read the script and they say 'please submit a budget', you submit them a budget, and they say 'yea' or 'nay', 'let's lower this', 'let's raise that' or here's the calendar – this is the number of weeks I want you to be on it'. Then you agree to a budget and you try your best to stick to that budget.

Unfortunately, because of what we do, and that includes picture editing and music and sound editing, it's not always an easy task to stick to the budget because so much of it is totally out of my control. I mean it's nothing I can personally control: I can't tell a director to stop making changes, I can't tell a director to stop cutting a picture, because if you are doing a film like an *Armageddon* or a *Godzilla*, whatever it might be, you can have a thousand sound elements per reel! So when the director goes in and makes fifty, sixty, a hundred picture changes all those elements have to be changed, and someone has to do it.

In my opinion that is probably the single biggest expense that a film goes through. The second one would be here in post-production. Now we seem to be working on an accelerated schedule: we dub on multiple stages at once, we pre-dub the dialogue on one stage, we pre-dub the sound effects on another, we might pre-dub the background and foley on another stage so that we can get it together quicker. It is also a budgetary issue because dubbing is very expensive, very expensive.

Sergi: Some designers have complained about the fact that post-production time has shrunk a lot for you.

Stambler: Yeah, it has shrunk ...

Sergi: Why is that? Is it just a matter of money? Or release times?

Stambler: I think the release times really dictate the schedules. I think the studios want to fill a particular hole in the schedule that they may have the opportunity to fill. You know, it is a smart business move for them: even though they may spend a little more money on one area because of the rush, or NOT spend it [laughs], at least they can get the film out there when they think it is best suited to go out, and the studios now are much more attuned to that than they used to be. A lot of that is dictated by previews – we have a lot of those – you know, marketing driven.

Sergi: When do you actually get called in on a job?

Stambler: You do it one or two ways. I always pretty much talk to the directors that I work with once every couple of months, some more than that.

Sergi: When a film is in development?

Stambler: All the time, I talk to them all the time anyway, just to talk to them. Because I am lucky, I have some really great people that I work with. I also look at the trades and see what's coming up, because they have pre-production in the trades, and I like to pick. If I don't have a movie that I am working on, I look at trades and say 'Oh, that looks like a good movie' and then I go AFTER that movie, and I try to get that movie. I'll write a letter, or call or get them a resume, see if there is anybody I know on it so that I can get an interview. Then I do the interview thing, if they hire you, do a budget, they approve the budget and then you get started on it. Then, basically, on most movies, I record location effects, go to wherever they are shooting, and I try to record every single scene that they are at, every location they go through.

Sergi: Why is that? Is that to get a sense of the place?

Stambler: Yeah, to get the ambience. Whenever you do something like that you always get good ideas and you haven't seen necessarily a frame of the movie. For a scene that is two minutes in the movie I'll record about two hours of sound for that location, because I'll go to every place. I always find very cool stuff that you wouldn't think of, that I never would think of, when I actually go there. It could be a number of things: for example we had a location and there was a very strange sound, I don't know what it was, there must have been a heater in the room or something. Every once in a while it would let out this 'whistle' which you never hear. I love that stuff. I love something different for me, and something different for the audience they have never heard of before.

Sergi: Do you try to do that consciously – trying to get 'new' sounds?

Stambler: Totally consciously.

Sergi: You go to the movies, listen to movies and say I'm going to do this ...

Stambler: Yeah

Sergi: Can you give me an example?

Stambler: A lot of it has to do with doing a lot of location recordings and the realism that it portrays. In a movie, that is much more real than building from your library. An example would be a movie I finished a little bit ago called *A Perfect Murder*. We went to New York to record some stuff and we ended up with FIFTY hours! But when you go to New York the sirens are very different than any other place you've ever been, very different, so we ended up going to Long Island in a police car and recording a lot of sirens sound. And those types of things you think of in the course of doing the movie, they just make it a lot more interesting.

Sergi: Let me be a little more specific. In particular, I'd like to talk about *The Fugitive*. In that film you almost get a sense that sound plays a more important role than the images ...

Stambler: It was like that in that movie. We had a great visual movie, but what we did with that movie was going over the top with sound, but tastefully, not ruining it. Actually, what we ended up doing is making much more of it then it deserved to be. I don't really mean 'deserved to be' but more of it than it's there. We took it to a different level, because basically it's a dialogue movie and we were just so into it. I get a real 'go for it' mentality in sound where I'm not really afraid to try anything. In that movie there was a lot of people that do this thing [Bruce turns his head suddenly as if startled by a sudden sound], that respond to things. So we purposely intensified that in every single sequence in a huge way, and we made as much of it as we possibly could.

Sergi: In the opening sequence, there are a lot of things that are not, talking about realism ...

Stambler: That are not real?

Sergi: Exactly

Stambler: We didn't want to do real. You know, a lot of it was driven by the picture editor because he's so damn good, Dennis Virkler, the guy is a genius. He was the picture editor also on *A Perfect Murder*. When you work with certain people in your job you are very careful to toe the line and if they say 'do x' you do x, you don't do x, y and z, because you are going get your ... you're going to get in trouble. Dennis Virkler and the producer Peter Macgregor Scott, here's what they say: 'GO for it, make it great'. You are not afraid to bring something new, but when you bring your material here [i.e. the dubbing stage] and there are fifteen, sixteen people watching you on the [dubbing] stage, you really are subject to quite a bit of ridicule, and you have to be able to take the good and the bad, you know [laughs]. We had a really 'go for it' attitude. It's a chemistry thing, you just accentuate everything.

Sergi: It's interesting that you mention the picture editor and the producer, but not the director [Andrew Davies]. Why is that?

Stambler: The director actually in my viewpoint has a little bit less of an input. They have more of an overview. For example, in *The*

Fugitive I personally struggled with the train crash. I examine every single element because the picture editor doesn't tell you necessarily all that it's happening in a scene; the director doesn't tell you either 'It's a train crash!' he'll say, and so will the producer 'It's a train crash!' but there is this series of shit that happens that makes the train crash. That's the way I think. I particularly struggled with the moment when the train derails off the tracks and then there is a shot in dirt of the train coming at you like this [Bruce simulates with his hand the movement of the train towards the audience]. I couldn't figure out how to do that. I'm into 'reality' effects. I'll process sounds but I want a base material to work from. So I got this big dumpster and I tied it to a truck with a 100-foot rope to it and towed it and then recorded the dumpster sliding. That is the kind of very detailed oriented material that goes into your film.

Sergi: At the beginning of the film there is a helicopter shot of Chicago. At one point, as the helicopter passes above a skyscraper, you can hear …

Stambler: … when the building swishes by [laughs]?

Sergi: Yes, that's it

Stambler: Yes, we did a lot buildings 'swish bys' [laughs].

Sergi: Where does that come from?

Stambler: Again, that's another example of 'I'm gonna do something for everything, have fun and make it very detail oriented'. Granted, no building is gonna swish by you, but if you were, say, to go by it, you would hear the air-conditioning. It is interesting, weird, subtle stuff that isn't too corny. Sound sucks you totally in. It sucks you in.

Sergi: Immediately after that scene, there is another interesting example. Usually in films there seems to be an unwritten rule: if you see it, you hear it. But in the murder scene visuals and sounds are very different [you see a woman being attacked and as she falls to the ground the sound she makes is not that of a body crushing on the floor but of a long, drained clap of thunder]. Where does that come from?

Stambler: It is a process of refinement. It's certainly did not start off that way. When you sit down and look at the film, you look at it over, and over, and over, and over again, and you want to stay away from too many 'like-sounds' in any given movie and kind of put a signature on stuff. We didn't want to use the sound of a head being cracked open, so you try different things.

Sergi: Did you show it to someone and they said 'Yeah, that works'?

Stambler: No, we just cut it.

Sergi: And nobody said 'No, I don't think it works'?

Stambler: Nobody did.

Sergi: Did you do lot of ADR [Automatic Dialogue Replacement] in the movie?

Stambler: I usually hire an ADR supervisor. In *The Fugitive* we did about 200 ADR lines.

Sergi: Not a lot then.

Stambler: No, but that's normal.

Sergi: Did you get it all in production?

Stambler: Most of it is production. I am much more a fan of production dialogue ...

Sergi: Why is that?

Stambler: Because ADR hardly ever matches, there could be synch issues, and can't be as original as production dialogue.

Sergi: However, isn't it true that many films add a lot of ADR in post-production?

Stambler: Yeah, you'll notice especially in films like *Lethal Weapon*, some people tend to fill every possible space with edited lines and off-screen dialogue. I think that's because they think the audience is not really bright. In *The Fugitive* we didn't do that.

Sergi: In that film there is one particular sound, the sound of police and ambulance sirens, that is scattered throughout the movie and works almost as an aural 'theme'. Was that a conscious choice?

Stambler: Totally conscious. For example, when the doctor comes out of the health club and we just hear a quick burst of a police siren, that scares the shit out of you [laughs]. We did that a lot. The siren sounds are mixed so that they are not repetitive. I just like to be conscious not to be repetitive and use the same sound too often.

Sergi: You didn't win an Oscar for that movie, but you won one for *The Ghost and the Darkness* ...

Stambler: ... which was a lot harder to make.

Sergi: Why is that?

Stambler: It was brutally hard, the hardest movie I've ever done, because of the lions. Animals are the hardest thing to do. Because I cannot use a real lion's growl, it just would not work. It's not threatening, etc. It's much more straightforward to do a dialogue movie with traffic and doors, etc., and then the next step would be a *Lethal Weapon*-type of movie with cars and explosions and car chases, that's also pretty straightforward. But from the level of difficulty animals are the worst, especially if they are major players in the movie. If there is any subtlety, or even more animals, then you are screwed, you really are. It's really hard, and it took me to the end. I think I was on the movie for eight months, and it took me about seven months to get the right lion sound! [laughs]. I went and recorded lions, tigers, bears, oh man, I must have over sixty hours' worth of animal recording. That's a lot of recording! A tiger is a great sound, and I have two trainers, one in LA and one in San Francisco. But animal trainers are not going to torture the tiger for you [laughs], because that's what they'd need to do to give me the kind of sound I'm looking for! Will they do that? Of course they won't do that! So you get all this material and then, can you guess what it is?

Sergi: Not in a million years.

Stambler: It's a combination of a bear, a tiger, and then a car. It's like a drag race car, you know how they rev? The rev is in there cut to the vocal …

Sergi: … and that's the lion?

Stambler: And that's the lion! It worked good though [laughs].

Sergi: The film went on to win an Academy Award for sound, which must mean that a lot of people thought it was a good soundtrack.

Stambler: Yes, it was good, I'm really proud of it.

Sergi: The question I'm leading to is what makes a good soundtrack? How do you know when it's 'good'?

Stambler: To my taste, one that has a lot of parameters in it. I thought that *Ghost* [*The Ghost and the Darkness*] had a lot of that; it was mixed really well. I thought it wasn't loud, that it wasn't painful, there's nothing that stood out and hurt you as a listener. That was a lot of detail, that the effects weren't too loud, that the music wasn't too loud, that you could hear all the dialogue, that it was creatively mixed and spread, released in the 6-track format. In that show those were the criteria. A movie is not your movie: you have a director and he is ultimately the one who calls the shots, but I personally am really anti-loud, I really hate it. These days movies are way too loud.

Sergi: An old bone of contention is that you must always hear the dialogue.

Stambler: Yeah, you must always be able to do that.

Sergi: But some directors in certain films seem to challenge that old view. In some films dialogue is also used to create pace, rhythm, and not so much for its literal value.

Stambler: Well, yes, but I think you should hear all the dialogue. In a movie you are trying to tell a story. The first thing you think if the dialogue can't be heard is 'I didn't hear what they said', and now you are no longer in the movie, period. You need to suck them in and keep them in.

Sergi: Is there a dialogue going on amongst sound men/women?

Stambler: Yeah, I especially talk to Gary [Rydstrom]. Sometimes you can't be absolutely sure that what you're doing is right. I remember when I was doing *The Ghost and the Darkness* I called Gary and asked him if he had any suggestions for the lion sounds. He said the same thing that I was thinking, 'Just throw it up there and see what works!', and I said 'Thanks a lot Gary!' [laughs]. And that's exactly what it is, when you are not really sure of something you need to keep trying different things and be open-minded. You know, digital has really helped that part. You can hear a lot of stuff together and that's really helped.

Sergi: In your opinion, what's the status of film sound today?

Stambler: I think it is more and more important. You know, I don't really care where my credit is at the end of the movie. I think that if sound is the responsibility not only of the supervising sound editor, but also of the sound team, and the director and a lot of times the end product will not necessarily reflect what could have been and what should have been, without being offensive to anybody. But the importance of sound is becoming much more prominent than it has been, especially in the past four, five years. They hire people like me and Gary and Randy Thom before they start shooting. They used to not do that until after the film was cut. They'd call you up and say 'Can you do this ...'. Also the credits are moving up. I think sound wasn't as important to film ten years ago, it really wasn't. I mean, there were shitty theatres everywhere, and now there are great theatres, especially here in LA. My son, who's 12, will go 'Dad, that movie was way too loud'. Yeah, I'm his daddy and he knows what he's talking about, but I think that audiences are much smarter today.

Sergi: You worked in TV. Lately, there has been a lot of good work in TV sound. What do you think of it?

Stambler: I don't really watch much TV. I only watch some video-tapes of the *X-Files*, but I don't watch it for sound. There is no doubt to me that the feature people are the top people. Period. I came from there, and I know how I thought [laughs].

Sergi: Is that the usual path to features, TV work?

Stambler: Yes, it is. But it is very difficult to get in. I've been work-ing with the same crew since *Under Siege*. My crew is great, and it is hard for someone to break into that calibre of a crew. Once you're happy with them you stick with them.

Sergi: Have you ever been unhappy with one of your films?

Stambler: I'd have to look at my resume! [laughs]. You can give up, because there is a whole political process that nobody knows, and it can be a very tricky and very delicate process. I did a Kevin Costner's movie [*The Postman*], a terrible movie, but, in my opin-ion, that movie sounded great. I didn't give up, like other people did, and you CAN give up, you can get people down.

Sergi: When you work with these big names, how much of their ego get in the way? How much do they understand about sound?

Stambler: They understand enough to 'like or not like' which is really all they need. What I like about people like that is that they say 'Do something great, I don't know what, just show me some-thing' and they'll say 'I want this to sound a bit dreamlike, see what you can come up with'. I know Joel [Schumaker] real good, it was my first time with Kevin [Costner] on *The Postman*, and as you work with people you learn to understand how they're com-municating. Because sound is a very arbitrary thing, very unspe-cific, and you have to think like they think, to get into their heads, to try and get their taste.

Sergi: That must be very difficult because some of the adjectives we use in everyday conversation are rather 'vague': the notion of what constitutes a 'threatening sound' might mean something totally different to two different people.

Stambler: Absolutely, and sometimes it is really hard to get what they want. It was really intimidating to me in the early part of my career. I used to go and sit down with the director and the picture editor to spot the movie and I'd pray to God nothing bad happened, that nothing really HARD happened! [pulls a face and laughs]. I mean, I used to get upset if a dog barked! It can get very difficult because people say 'Oh, that's the wrong dog' or 'that's not in synch'. There can be a thousand of those things that can haunt you. When I work on a picture I'm on it 24 hours a day, I'm always thinking about it when there are any unresolved issues. I walk around, I hear something cool, I'm gonna get my recorder! I don't know what I'm going to use it for, but I know I will.

Sergi: How big is your sound library?

Stambler: Very big, it's huge. It must be around 40,000 hours.

Sergi: How do you catalogue all that?

Stambler: There's a special computer program that tells you everything. You pull up a 'lion' sound, and it'll tell you all about that 'lion': who it was shot by, when, where, for what, etc.

Sergi: Do you keep updating your library constantly?

Stambler: Yeah, constantly, on every movie. Some movies not as much as others. Some movies you might do 10 hours, some movies you might 60/70 hours.

Sergi: At present you are working with six channels. However, the voice is always in the centre channel.

Stambler: Yeah, principal dialogue is always in the centre channel. Because if you put the dialogue in another channel your audience will do this [Bruce turns around as if trying to figure out where that line of dialogue has been spoken from]. For me that's another unwritten rule, like the one about understanding dialogue.

Sergi: But for the rest of the soundtrack you can do whatever you want.

Stambler: Put it wherever you want: you can pan it, you can put it in the surround, you are free to do whatever you want. You can be as creative as you dare to be.

Sergi: How about the use of the surround channel?

Stambler: This is interesting in relation to what you were suggesting before about the differences between LA and New York [this refers to a previous part of our conversation where I suggested that the locality where a movie is mixed can have a substantial influence on the way that movie will sound]. I really like some of the work that comes out of New York. I've been to Sound One [one of New York's leading sound facilities], I love some of their work. I personally think this is the result of dubbing in small rooms. They dub in very small rooms. I mean, they are tiny rooms compared to this room. I think by virtue of that hardly any of those films have any surround at all. All LA-based films, not all of them, but most of them have a lot of surrounds and boom; you won't find much boom coming out of New York either. I think part of that is because of the dubbing environment. I also think that some re-recording mixers, I know that for a fact, are more timid than others, and that's true with us too. *The Fugitive* was 'out there' from a sound point of view, but we had Franky Montagno as our sound effects mixer, and to me Franky is the best sound effects mixer on the planet, he is just as good as Gary [Rydstrom].

Sergi: Would you ever use the surround channels to give primary information to the audience?

Stambler: Yeah, I would. I wouldn't NOT do anything. I'd go for anything if it worked. You just have to keep an open mind and then see how it works in proximity to the rest of the scene. I think that creatively you go for it, you have nothing to lose, and certainly when you are in an environment to try anything. Again, it is a matter of some money and extra dubbing time and all that.

Sergi: When you read a script do you mind the fact that there isn't much, if any, information about what kind of sound is expected?

Stambler: No, not really. I don't read scripts as much as I used to because they tend to make me feel either disappointed or too happy as to what I end up working with. Of course, sometimes reading them helps me understand the story better, but I tend not to [laughs].

Sergi: So what do you work on, a treatment?

Stambler: If I'm in the process of bidding for a show I read the script, but if I can get around not reading it, I won't worry. Then I'll get a tape of the movie and work from that. It's just like when you've read the book and then you see the movie, it's just like that [laughs].

Sergi: Sound has come a long way in the past twenty years. Some people have called this the 'second coming of sound'. How would you describe the developments that have taken place in this period from your perspective?

Stambler: What you call the 'second coming of sound' I call the coming of sound, period! [laughs], because we didn't really have sound. We pretty much had dialogue and had a centre speaker and that was it. But now theatres have spent [a] huge amount of dollars upgrading their sound equipment. It's amazing to me that we would dub in a theatre and then it would almost be so close to what we have done harmonically in a room filled with people! And there are no limits. So it's just a case of not overpowering the picture but complementing it, not being too loud, and involving the audience as much as we can.

Sergi: Where do you see sound going in the near future?

Stambler: I don't know. I suppose you could have vibrating seats and stuff like that. You could literally do anything you wanted, but I suppose it still depends on the visuals.

Sergi: Is it still a visual medium?

Stambler: My thinking still takes a backseat to what I see. I will go the extra mile as in a movie like *The Fugitive* provided that the visuals and the subject matter support it. But a lot of movies don't do that.

Note

1   See www.soundstorm.com (accessed 1 March 2003).

2

Tackling sound: suggestions for sound analysis

Textual analysis is an important tool for film scholars. This is true both in an interpretative framework and in a more inclusive approach as a means to study the dynamics at work in the relationship between audiences, movies and their makers. Indeed, textual analysis has played a crucial role in, at the very least, legitimising some of the most influential theoretical currents in film studies.[i] However, despite its continuous influence, textual analysis has been remarkably impervious to all things sound. Although the vocabulary we employ to analyse images in movies is far from being completely satisfactory, the confidence that it has generated in scholars has helped to produce countless examples of 'visual' textual analysis. The same cannot be said of sound. The most obvious sign of this bias is the notion of *mise-en-scène*. This established way of (literally) looking at movies takes into account some core aspects of filmmaking, such as acting, lighting, framing and costume. In less 'strict' interpretations of *mise-en-scène* scholars have included other aspects, such as camerawork, but have routinely disregarded sound as central to the close analysis of a film. It is my aim in this chapter to identify and indicate some areas of film soundtracks that I believe might yield useful questions about the way sound works in films. In this sense, I am more interested in analysing sound in film in terms of practices and dynamics and less as a means to ascertain 'meaning'. For someone who claims such a 'bias' I am exposed to challenges about the actual possibility of separating those two acts, since they are central practices in my own profession. Nevertheless, the 'political' project here remains one that hopes to move away from a straightforward investigation of how meaning is constructed so as to help understand more about the surface of movies produced in the

Dolby era. This is not to suggest that previous to this period sound was not worthy of attention, or that most of my arguments apply exclusively to contemporary cinema, but rather to emphasise the level of complexity and exuberance that film sound has achieved in the period I am dealing with.

Several scholars – Chion, Altman, Bordwell and Thompson amongst others – have contributed to a greater understanding of how sound works with a number of significant attempts at developing a terminology of sound. Indeed, I should speak of sound terminologies, given the richness and variety of these attempts.[2] Although these terms and concepts are instrumental to the development of film sound scholarship, the nature of their project is to illustrate individual instances of sound. That is, they provide scholars and students with analytical tools at a 'micro-level', but they rarely address the investigative framework, the 'macro-level' of sound aesthetics, within which those terms and concepts could function organically. When Bordwell and Thompson speak of diegetic and non-diegetic sound, to name but one famous example, they are more concerned with specific instances of sound in a film and less with how sound functions overall in any given movie. I believe this lack of a structural framework to be one of the key reasons why, despite so many interesting examples of sound vocabularies, most scholars still show uneasiness when attempting to incorporate sound in their analysis of movies. Thus, my main aim here is to provide a first level of 'macro' sound analysis.

It is a common enterprise to dissect films in ways that attempt to reproduce lab work: scholars will take a movie or a sequence and will watch it several times in conditions they assume are best suited to reveal whatever insight into filmmaking they are seeking. Textual analysis is the most classic of these examples. Michel Chion, to name one famous example, puts forward his suggestions for a macro-analysis of sound in the last chapter of his *Audio-Vision* entitled 'Introduction to Audiovisual Analysis'.[3] Chion suggests the process he calls 'masking' (i.e. turning attention to either sound or image whilst masking the other element out from viewing or hearing) as a central strategy to sound analysis. He suggests that

> The trickiest stage of the masking procedure involves listening to the sound by itself, acousmatically. Technically, this must be done in a relatively dead sound environment that is well isolated from outside noise conditions which must be carefully arranged. Second, participants must

be willing to concentrate. We are not at all used to listening to sounds, especially non-musical sounds, to the exclusion of anything else.[4]

Chion here assumes that his implied readership of film scholars will accept this 'quasi-scientific' approach as a necessary evil. I must confess that I am tempted to adopt the same strategy (and, indeed, I am 'guilty as charged' in parts of this study). However, there are problems that arise from this commonly used methodology and they all revolve around the question of audiences. Chion's suggested approach mostly disregards the experience of ordinary audiences who are in a position that is diametrically opposite to the one he suggests. Their everyday experience of cinema, our everyday experience of cinema, is one that is strongly dependent on a variety of conditions outside our direct control. We cannot be sure that the theatre we will be sitting in will have perfect insulation from adjacent theatres or even from the outside world, and that its instrumental equipment will be rendered acoustically neutral (these elements, as I outlined in a previous article on cinema audiences, constitute what I have termed the 'structural soundtrack').[5] Even if we were in the 'perfect theatre' (and agreeing on what constitutes such a thing would require much debating), we would still have to contend with other members of the audience (i.e. the 'audience soundtrack'), whose aural contribution to the film experience cannot simply be bypassed. Secondly, Chion chooses to ignore the fact that filmmakers do not design sound for the kind of audience experience he suggests. Indeed, the process of final mixing, as any account of filmmaking practices will confirm, relies on two core notions that are based on exactly the opposite premise:

1   The power of sound in creative terms depends on the immediacy of the experience, the 'here and now' of the film experience. Audiences cannot spend too much time thinking about sound (or the image for that matter) and that transient, momentary nature of the act of seeing and hearing is what makes the illusion of cinema work.
2   Audiences do not inhabit an ideally standardised audiovisual space, but rather a pale version of it (hence witness the amount of money and resources that studios and film companies have poured into the search for improving standards of reproduction).

I believe that greater consideration needs to be given to filmmaking practices, that it is important to develop a method of analysis that favours the investigation of what sound does, not what it should do, and that 'everyday audiences' should be seen as central to this project. This is not to devalue the importance of close analysis, but to reposition it in a wider context as a tool for analysis, not *the* tool. It might be useful in this sense to lay down clearly the foundations upon which my suggestions for sound analysis are based. There are three key features that describe my approach: inclusive, medium-specific and contemporary. The approach I am about to suggest is inclusive in the sense that it attempts to move away from the concept of individual authorship and takes more into account the complex web of relationships at work in any given contemporary soundtrack. It would be tempting to focus on the body of work of individual sound designers such as Walter Murch, Gary Rydstrom, Ben Burtt or Dane Davies as 'authors of sound'. Indeed, this is partly inevitable for they are the most interviewed and written-about people and their views and ideas recur more often than others do. However, this need not amount to a redressing of auteurism as it could easily hinder our understanding of the dynamics at work in the creation of a soundtrack, not to mention its relationship with audiences. The views and work of sound men and women in Hollywood are central to my approach but only insofar as they serve the 'greater good' of understanding how sound works. Secondly, this approach wishes to be medium specific in that it needs to overcome some established notions of film sound that have been particularly limiting in their vague attention to film's own specificity. The most obvious example of how 'unspecific' textual analysts have been in relation to sound is the rather vague and often contradictory vocabulary that has been employed over the years. As I have previously discussed, to conflate the terms 'music' and 'soundtrack', to name but one example, is to betray the fact that the former is part of the latter, and not vice versa. Consequently, even the most basic question 'what is a film soundtrack?' has often been taken erroneously for granted. This remains as much a conceptual problem as it is one of language. Finally, it is a contemporary approach. Historically, most versions of textual analysis and *mise-en-scène* were formed and hardened into film studies in the 1960s and early 1970s. Crucially, this was before the exponential increase in the interest on and investment in film sound by both industry and consumer took place.[6] Moreover, political hostility towards Hollywood heavily characterised debates and critical thinking at the time. The immediate consequence of this is that established concepts that we routinely employ to carry out sound analysis are, literally, outdated. Contemporary soundtracks are neither intrinsically better nor worse than the ones that preceded such a seismic change, but they are significantly more complex. This is true in relation to both filmmaking practices and audience reception, as these words from Murch emphasise:

> The general level of complexity ... has been steadily increasing over the seven decades since film sound was invented. And starting with Dolby Stereo in the 1970s, continuing with computerized mixing in the 1980s and various digital formats in the 1990s, that increase has accelerated even further. Sixty years ago, for instance, it would not be unusual for an entire film to need only fifteen to twenty sound effects. Today that number could be hundreds to thousands of times greater.[7]

Ultimately the approach I am outlining revolves as much around considerations of context as of text. As I hope this study has proven thus far, any attempt at understanding how sound works in the Dolby era, indeed in any era, has to deal with issues such as attitudes, projected audience, established views, and assumptions. It is for this reason that I have structured the first part of this suggested framework as a series of brief questions and issues directly addressed to the reader. I am assuming, and as with all assumptions I am aware of the risk that this entails, that primarily student and scholars of film will read this study. That is whom I refer to when I say 'we' or 'us'. I would also like to state the obvious and emphasise that although there are similarities amongst different movies in terms of how sound is employed, there are also substantial differences depending on a variety of factors, including issues concerning production (the composition of the film crew), time (release dates), and money (budget). In other words, what I am suggesting is a tool for investigating sound, not a template of what contemporary soundtracks 'ought to sound like'.

For a more organic approach – part one: a question of attitude

I suggest that before carrying out any attempt at analysing (and evaluating) the way sound functions in any given film it is crucial to address a few concerns and ask some basic questions. I offer these in no specific order, as I believe them all to be important.

On audiences

What audience are you going to have in mind when writing? Is it the 'ideal audience' Chion engages with, or the 'unstructured' audience who inhabits your local theatre? Clearly, this is a rather incomplete choice I am offering you (is there such a thing as an 'ordinary' audience?), but it is a central choice nonetheless. If the audience we have in mind is an ideal audience, capable of detecting every subtle instance of film sound, impervious to extraneous noises and distractions, and uniformly predisposed to constant attention, then we do not need to concern ourselves with conditions of reception in film theatres (or at home), nor do we need to account for other differences (in cultural references, hearing patterns, age). However, if you wish to account for a less 'ideal' kind of audience, then the issue of the dynamics of a soundtrack, as well as conditions of reception, become much more important. To name but one example: there are some choices that cannot be noticed by audiences for they happen at such a subtle level that there is no time for the audience to register them. The sound of Erin Brockovich's car slowing down to a gentle 'purr' to enhance the mood of the scene when she has just been told that her baby daughter has just spoken her first word cannot be noticed in itself – its effectiveness is in the overall mix.[8] On the other hand, any gun sound employed in *Terminator 2* stands out in its own right and demands to be noticed. One works because it is not noticed, the other because it is; one chooses shadows, the other steps into the limelight. It is not a matter of value or effectiveness: both strategies can be very effective.

On research

It should be obvious at this stage in my study that I value accounts of filmmakers' practices in creating sound as much as I appreciate the importance of academic literature. Indeed, a synthesis of the two ought to be seen as central to my enterprise. However, most traditional accounts of film sound (indeed, of film at large) have mostly eschewed any attempt at incorporating filmmakers' voices and have elected academia as the core of their investigation. Although this is perfectly understandable (indeed the same attitude is true of most filmmakers, who have often regarded academic accounts of film sound as 'alien' and 'irrelevant'), many scholars, myself included, have in the past chosen to employ this artificial division between theory and practice as a comforting 'buffer zone' between academia and the filmmaking community. This is a very important issue in relation to the kind of attitude you are likely to adopt in your research. One of the few advantages that sound scholars have enjoyed as a direct consequence of the 'lesser status' of the discipline is that sound men and women are much more open and willing to talk about their art and craft than other, more established aspects of filmmaking. Thus, it is reasonable to assume that exchanging views with filmmakers is a real possibility for scholars, and indeed a choice to be considered when writing about sound.[9]

On budgets

The gap between low-budget movies and big-budget movies is not as wide as one might logically assume. Sound need not be a tremendously expensive part of filmmaking, assuming (and this is a big assumption) that planning is carried out properly. In this sense, good communication and collaboration between producer, director, picture editor and supervising sound editor is crucial in order to avoid needless time wasting. Undoubtedly, would-be blockbusters will have substantially larger budgets than any low-budget, or even average, film production. However, precisely because of the money and expectations involved, this will often translate into less time for post-production (mostly because of the need to hit a specific release date to maximise profit and avoid head-to-head confrontations with other big-budget films) and greater pressure on sound crews. Indeed, the shrinking of time allowed to the sound crew in post-production from the mid-1980s onwards is an issue that filmmakers often indicate as a serious threat to sound quality.[10] Most importantly, most sound men and women approach sound making with much the same attitude, be it for a run-of-the-mill movie or the latest blockbuster. In this sense, it is interesting to note how most leading designers in Hollywood occasionally work on 'small' projects.[11]

On technology

What is the place that technology occupies in your research? This question refers to a particularly limiting dichotomy, once again arising from auteurist notions of creativity. Many scholars have correctly emphasised the role that radio mikes and multi-track mixing have played in helping Robert Altman achieve the rather unique style of sound that characterise most of his movies.[12] However, rather than seeing this as one of many instances of how sound technology can empower filmmakers when they are open to the possibilities that technology can offer, Altman's example has often been indicated as the exception that confirms the rule. This false dichotomy between (passive) technology and (active) creativity is an obstacle to our evaluation of the central role that technology plays, not only in sound, but also in cinema at large. Technology empowers as much as it shapes (and hence, limits) filmmakers' creativity.

On creativity

This issue is a further extension of the previous question on technology. Most scholarly attitudes towards sound, as we have seen, understand sound to be a technical part of filmmaking, creativity being located elsewhere in the filmmaking process. In my opinion, this is perhaps the most damaging of all common assumptions about sound for it cripples our ability to investigate fully the creative effort involved in making film sound. To consider sound as a button-pushing, knob-tweaking exercise is to limit the scope of our research to investigating only those same aspects. Important though these may be, the huge creative effort that goes on before and after those buttons are pushed remains an unknown quantity in film sound. As Gary Rydstrom points out, there are people who

> Have deemed the sound world of filmmaking to be strictly technical, as if it was negative cutting. Of course, it isn't, and the best filmmakers know it isn't and make use of it. The danger is that, if you think something is just technical you are ignoring the artistic capabilities of it and so directors do it at their peril if they think that it is a technical exercise. Sound people themselves, I think, suffer from the idea that it is simpler than it really is, that there isn't great potential for creative use of the soundtrack.[13]

On sound vs. image

Another important question to arise from considerations of creativity is whether you believe the image to have inherently greater power of creative expression than sound. I recall a colleague who, in the question-and-answer session after his paper at a conference on Hollywood cinema, confidently stated that images are more complex than sounds. This is a central issue because, once again, it is a matter of intellectual attitude: if you believe that the image is creatively the more important force within a movie, indeed, that it possesses greater expressive powers, you are mostly likely to approach

sound in a negative fashion. Elisabeth Weis has perfectly captured
the pitfalls inherent to this problem as early as 1978.[14] In an article
she wrote on Hitchcock's use of sound, she says

> In a famous attack on Alfred Hitchcock's work, Penelope Houston
> complained that in *The Birds* 'most of the menace [comes] from the
> electronic soundtrack, to cover the fact that the birds are not really
> doing their stuff' … Miss Houston's comment is representative in its
> implication that Hitchcock's use of film sound is a 'poor relation' to
> his manipulation of the image. The belief that aural techniques are a
> means of expression inferior to visual ones is shared by most film
> scholars and, indeed, by many filmmakers.[15]

On filmmakers

The Directors Guild of America considers sound a technical category and thus prohibits head credits be given to sound.[16] This is not
merely an issue of 'ego'. Film sound has a problem with status within
the filmmaking community, as much as it has within the academic
community. In this sense, Randy Thom's remarks about directors
'treating sound as a necessary evil, and afterthought, or whipping
boy'[17] reveal the political struggle sound men and women need to
fight on most jobs. This struggle involves all aspects of film: from not
considering sound early enough in the production process to allo-
cating insufficient times during post-production, from considering
sound as 'technical' to employing sound as merely a support to the
image. Conditions of labour are thus important because they may
provide us with an important insight into the creative process of a
film. The suggestion that the final mix is a process whereby sound
crews execute the director's vision is an empty statement partly born
out of the belief that film production is a 'standardised' process. The
reality is that the degree of creative input and choice that sound
people will be allowed varies tremendously according to who is in
charge of the overall movie project. Obviously, there will be many
instances where to research these issues will be extremely difficult, if
not unfeasible, even for the most enterprising of scholars. However,
to ignore these issues and treat each movie as if conditions of production were always the same is simply another way of bypassing
questions of filmmaking practice altogether.

Issues and questions such as the ones above are crucial because
they can help us confront those deep-rooted fears about sound
by (re)evaluating issues of production, technological choice (and

limitation), creative processes, conditions of labour, before we take on assessing how sound contributes to any given film. If nothing else, they can help inject a healthy dose of self-doubt in even the most image-conscious scholar.

For a more organic approach – part two: sound dynamics

I have articulated my thinking in this section around the concept of sound design. The latter is here used in the wider acceptance of the term as the process of arranging sound objects and spaces to produce an overall effect, not just in terms of 'creating' new sounds. In this sense, the role of the sound designer can be most usefully compared to that of the production designer: some filmmakers, like Murch, have indicated the director of photography as their 'visual' equivalent. However, as a three-dimensional construct I believe sound to be closer to production design than cinematography, both in conceptual and physical terms.[18] Within the overall concept of design, there are elements that can help structure our thinking about how sound works in any given movie. I would like to begin by suggesting four groupings that can help us explore individual issues. Once again, there is no particular hierarchy amongst these headings. They are: orchestration, contrast, focus and definition.

On orchestration
The concept of sound orchestration is a good starting point simply because it is the most macroscopic of all four groups. It involves developing an overall impression of how the soundtrack of a given film articulates a series of key relationships. One obvious starting point is the balance between the four different elements in a soundtrack. Virtually all movies will have a proportion of music, dialogue, sound effects and silence.[19] Interestingly, most attention in existing critical literature has focused on cinema's 'voco-centrism', that is, the special attention that is given to the voice over the other elements of the soundtrack.[20] Although it is true that dialogue intelligibility will take precedence over other elements in the soundtrack, this does not nullify the issue of choice: how these four elements are combined will vary tremendously between different movies. A film such as *Magnolia* relies more on a very complex combination of music and dialogue, and less on sound effects and silence. Conversely, *The Right Stuff* has a much greater balance between all four

elements. There is no intrinsic value in either approach for clearly the possible permutations are almost limitless. The question of whether the specific chosen approach works is to be considered within the confines of the narrative of that movie, especially in the case of filmmakers who have shown a sophisticated approach to sound in their movies.

A further aspect of orchestration is the relationship between front and rear channels, what I call the 'aesthetics of surround'. Contemporary film sound is defined by multi-channel technology. Again, almost all mainstream movies made in Hollywood over the period I am considering were released in one or more multi-channel system (analogue in the late 1970s and 1980s, digital from the 1990s onwards). This means that sound men and women have the choice of sourcing sound from a variety of points around the theatre. Indeed, the proliferation of channels available has not stopped since the beginning of the Dolby era: from the original $3+1$ (i.e. Dolby Stereo's three front channels and one rear channel for surround sound) we have progressed to the present $3+2$ (DTS and Dolby Digital), $5+2$ (SDDS in its full configuration) and $3+3$ (Dolby Labs and Lucasfilm's latest development, Dolby EX). In other words, the 'balance' of sound between front and rear does not *have* to be heavily weighted towards the front, that is, towards the screen. That this should still be the case in so many movies is a choice, not a necessity, and this clearly has consequences in the way sound functions within the overall project of a movie. Some movies, for example *Forrest Gump*, use the rear channels sparsely (see the case study on *Forrest Gump* on page 156). Others make heavy use of it – for example, in *The Remains of the Day* it emphasises the many 'hidden' areas of the house at the core of the narrative as well as providing audiences with a sense of 'geography' within the house (how big, where we are, and so on). Ordinarily, Hollywood movies still rely heavily on the front channels, in what I call the 'one-wall narrative approach' (see Chapter 1). However, some designers – Dane Davis (*The Matrix*) and Gary Rydstrom (*Saving Private Ryan*, *Strange Days*) – amongst others, have been rather more willing to explore the potential of the surround channels. This is not just an issue of 'putting effects or music in the surround'. Surround sound has the potential of expressing levels of narrative that confirm, contradict or simply differ from what the front channels suggest. Dolby EX has now placed rear and front channels on an almost equal level: front channel speakers still have greater dynamic range than surround speakers (although this is more a consequence of established practice than technological limitations) and, obviously, front channels can rely on being the 'screen channels'. However, the present situation is very different from that of mono sound or even early stereo when the imbalance in favour of front channels was all too evident and limiting. In other words, the possibility for greater articulation of the relationship between front and rear sound is available to sound designers, and their taking up this 'challenge' is partly dependent on being able to break down old established views as to what 'works' with audiences. Greater critical attention to this issue might help filmmakers in this sense.

There is, of course, another aspect to the issue of orchestration that I do not wish to take for granted. The availability of a technology does not make that technology inescapable: mixing films in stereo is still a choice. Indeed, just as silence makes sense only in a world of sound, the choice of mono makes even more sense in today's world of multi-channel technology. Over the years, some filmmakers have chosen mono for some of their movies for a variety of reasons. Most recently, *Traffic* was mostly mixed in mono, music aside. When I asked Larry Blake, the supervising sound editor on the movie, about it he confirmed that this was a conscious choice in order to highlight the 'documentary' feel of the movie. Similarly, Martin Scorsese and Frank Warner adopted a similar approach for *Raging Bull*, where most of the movie is mixed in mono. That is to say, mono is still a choice, much as black and white can still be chosen over colour cinematography. Interestingly, this should not be seen exclusively as a technical matter of whether only one channel is used. The concept of mono also refers to mixing style: some filmmakers might use directionality and surround to widen narrative space as widely as possible, whereas others may prefer to keep the sound 'smaller' and restrict sound space in much the same way they may choose to 'restrict' image exuberance (just think of techniques such as overexposing the picture, as indeed is the case in some instances in *Traffic*, or 'washing it out' of all colour to give it a kind of silver-bathed look as in *Se7en*). Ultimately, the concept of orchestration is useful to establish early on in the investigation of a soundtrack the relative weighting and role that each element will have. In this sense, questions of whether a hierarchy of sounds is discernibly central to the way the film is narrated can help understand the creative process involved.

On contrast

The complexity of most soundtracks requires a great deal of preparation before sound and images are married together in the final
mix. When done properly, preparation can help filmmakers' thinking about a particular sequence by, for example, deciding how to
break down that sequence in terms of sound effects, music, and so
on. Preparation can also save time in the final mix, and that can
mean big money savings. The most important process in this sense
is pre-mixing. This is a process where the sounds that a given
sequence require are broken down into 'stems' or groups of sounds
that can then be mixed to the picture individually. The purpose of
this process is to get to the final mix with as much material as possible already mixed and ready to be married to the picture. What is
relevant here is that sound is composed sequence by sequence. This
means that in order for it to work over time, filmmakers need to
keep control over their material across sequences as well as within
sequences. In other words, there is material that needs arranging
within each sequence, but this also needs to be done with an overall
understanding of how it should all play once all sequences are sewn
together. The concept of 'contrast' can help us investigate this aspect
of film sound.

Once a rough cut of the process of selecting the different sounds
that will go in each sequence is completed (I will talk more in detail
about the process of selecting the material that goes into each
sequence when I discuss the concept of 'focus'), filmmakers will have
to deal with several sequences, all potentially sounding different, for
each will have its own ambience and dynamics. The way these different sequences play against each other provides possibility for contrast: some sequences might have a quiet ambience with little sound
playing at low level whereas others might have great density and be
played at full throttle. The way these different ambiences are contrasted against one another is a good place to investigate how sound
works in a film. An excellent example of how contrast can be used
effectively comes from *Alien*. The crew of the *Nostromo* is awak-
ened prematurely from their deep sleep to answer what appears to
be an SOS call from an unknown planet. An away team is assembled
and sent to the planet's surface to investigate. At this point, the narrative calls for a mismatch to be created in terms of the two environments: the (safe) ship the humans inhabit and the (unsafe)
planet's surface. In the soundtrack, the contrast between the outside

space of the planet and the comforts of the ship's interior is clearly established with the creation of two completely different ambiences (contrast in the soundtrack is rendered all the more effective through picture editing by alternating shots between the ship and the planet's surface). Although both spaces are in the dark, save from a few artificial lights, sonically the two environments are opposites. The ship's interior is both weather-controlled and sonically insulated: the gentle 'whirring' of the chair of one of the crew members aboard ship moving slowly into position works to emphasise this 'quiet quality'. The planet's surface, on the other hand, is raged by continuous thunderstorms of great ferocity and deafening force: members of the away team on the surface need to shout to make themselves heard over the roaring winds. It is not a matter of loudness alone: the planet surface sounds deafening because it is contrasted with the virtually silent ship interior. In this sense, contrast can also happen over a whole movie to establish an aural theme: in *Forrest Gump* (see more on page 156) the ambience of Forrest's home works as an aural theme and it plays against the various ambiences of the places and times Forrest goes through in his 'journey'.

Contrast can also be used within a sequence to shape it dynamically. Towards the end of *Saving Private Ryan*, a small group of American soldiers is enjoying a rare moment of, literally, peace and quiet. Indeed, some of them find a gramophone and begin listening to an Edith Piaf song. Amongst rubble and destruction (the sequence takes place in a destroyed town), the melody echoes through the buildings, permeating the moment with a rather harmonious ambience. However, as the men begin relaxing into the moment, a strident, metallic distant sound is heard as German tanks approach the town. Here the shift in sound within the same ambience signals the end of one stage of the movie and the beginning of the next. There is no need for loud explosions, nor any point-of-view shot of German troops advancing being spotted by the American soldiers: aural contrast does it simply and effectively. Here contrast works both within the soundtrack and between image and sound, as the contrast between Piaf's song and the rubble that surrounds the characters creates a powerful mixture of emotions: peace amidst destruction. Perhaps the most revealing aspect of the notion of contrast comes if we look at it from the perspective of 'sound happening over time'. As Gary Rydstrom points out (see full interview on page 163) 'sounds are always playing in relation to what came before and what came after ... You think in terms of the whole picture in coming up with these sounds'. Clearly, this is not a new phenomenon, nor is it a domain of Hollywood movies: Robert Bresson once suggested that 'Against the tactics of speed, of noise, set tactics of slowness, of silence.'[21]

On focus

If filmmaking is a matter of choices, sound is no exception. Nowhere is this more evident and relevant than in the creative process involved in organising sound within a sequence. Each sequence in a movie will have a certain number of sound elements: individual sound effects (such as the sound of cars, trains, guns, explosions, breathing, water flowing, etc.), voices (dialogue, background voices, etc.), music (incidental, non-incidental, orchestral, solo, etc.), foley (footsteps, rustling of paper, etc.) and, as a consequence of the way these elements are arranged, silence (emphasised by the distant humming of a ship's engine, the gentle breeze of a summer evening, etc.). The concept of 'focus' can help investigate the articulation of these elements as well as identify the selection process that it is inevitably involved. A simple example might help. Imagine this sequence: it is Christmas time. A man walks purposefully through a busy shopping mall in search of someone. He enters some shops, peers through the windows of others and never even stops for breath. Finally he realises that he has come full circle; whoever he is looking for is not there. He walks back to the parking lot and drives off to continue his search elsewhere. If the sound crew were to decide to fill this sequence with all the possible sounds that could be heard they would need hundreds, possibly thousands of sound elements. Think of all the different ambiences of each shop as well as the overall sound-scape of the mall: add the sounds coming from the hundreds (thousands?) of people busy shopping for Christmas: busy chatter, children screaming, people arguing, couples laughing, etc. Now include the typical Christmas music fare: bells, choirs, Santa's Grotto and the like. Do not forget the 'mechanical' aspects of the sequence: heating vents, tills ringing, automatic doors opening and closing. Once you have done all this, add all the echoes, reverb and distant sound that would fill a space as large and as busy as a shopping mall at Christmas. To include all these elements in this (rather brief) scene I described would be both unwise and impossible for reasons that are both perceptual and conceptual. There is a point where adding another sound element, no matter how small, will cloud the clarity of an existing sound. Soon the clarity of the whole sequence will be compromised and cacophony is all that the audience will be left with. In perceptual terms, sounds covering the same frequency will simply cancel each other out: three children screaming will form a screaming 'group' (or, as it is commonly known, a layer); adding twenty more screaming children to that layer will not improve the 'screaming' quality of the layer, but it will most likely reduce its clarity.[22] In other words, it will sound just as loud but less distinctive. In conceptual terms, too many sound layers will produce a kind of conceptual cacophony: they will end up sounding like a mass of sound whose individual components are not distinguishable. This issue is rightly considered of paramount importance amongst filmmakers. Murch has been the most eloquent in this sense for he has coined what he calls the 'Two-and-a-half things' law, according to which he organises sound elements:

> There is a rule of thumb I use which is never to give the audience more than two-and-a-half things to think about aurally at any one moment. Now, those moments can shift very quickly, but if you take a five-second section of sound and feed the audience more than two-and-a-half conceptual lines at the same time, they can't really separate them out. There's just no way to do it, and everything becomes self-canceling.[23]

Clearly, we would not simply be able to piece together all the sounds in the mall sequence and make them magically work together. The relevant considerations here then become what elements to use in the sequence (how many sound elements, of what 'kind'), but also what to leave out. We will also need to decide what elements will drive the sequence in the foreground, and what elements will work better in the background. Ultimately the combination of all these elements works to 'focus' audience attention to specific sounds and to specific combinations of those sounds, and that is why it is important to investigate the issue of focus. Every movie, and every sequence within that movie, will have a certain degree of density and clarity. A film like *Magnolia* is very dense, with only a few instances where that density is mitigated. As we discussed about contrast, this can be made to work to the film's advantage: the few moments where sound is used sparsely work to highlight the dense moments in the movie. On the other hand, a film might use little density for most of its duration so that when a 'peak' is reached density can be increased accordingly to emphasise that moment in the narrative. In a horror movie such as *Halloween* it is customary to have a relatively sparse soundtrack, other than the moments where an attack takes place. Then the sudden and substantial increase in sound density will help jolt the audience.

What is important to bear in mind here is that, as in the case of orchestration and contrast, there are no rules, other than those of physics and human perception in terms of what 'works' when it comes to focus. Ultimately, the combination of density and the degree of clarity that filmmakers might want to achieve is only one of many combinations that could 'work' for any given narrative. Nor does clarity mean being able to hear everything all the time: the lack of clarity in a sequence could work to the film's advantage. In *Blade Runner*, Deckard (the character played by Harrison Ford) chases one of the female replicants across the streets of a futuristic Los Angeles. The sequence is incredibly dense with several dozens of sound elements all playing at full throttle. The result is cacophony. However, that is precisely the way the characters involved experience the city environment in the narrative. Indeed, Scott and his sound crew use this level of density and lack of clarity to contrast the much quieter moments when the characters are above street level (in the case of Deckard's apartment, for example), as Graham Hartstone, the sound mixer on *Blade Runner*, emphasises: 'Ridley always wanted energy. He never wanted the energy level of the track to drop. He created this horrendous environment in the future in this city full of pollution and he wanted noise pollution to be there all the time as well to keep you on the edge of your seat.'[24] In contrast, a scene in *The Conversation* that could potentially be very dense and have little clarity (a busy city square) employs a rather sparse soundtrack with a great degree of clarity (indeed, Harry Caul's search for aural clarity is perhaps 'the' central theme of the movie). In both instances, the filmmakers' choice of the combination of density and clarity work to focus audience attention: to the violent, discordant nature of the crowded streets that the characters inhabit in *Blade Runner*, and to the very personal world of a man whose life is spent 'eavesdropping' on other people in *The Conversation*. Thinking about focus is thus very important because it helps highlight the need for filmmakers to achieve some kind of 'order' in what could potentially otherwise be irreversibly chaotic. This aspect is crucial in terms of the final heading: definition.

On definition

To investigate aural definition is to ask questions about what sounds are emphasised, how they work, what kind of interplay is created with other sounds. The choices that filmmakers need to make in terms of what to focus on are defined by the specific sounds to which audience attention is to be directed. In particular, there are sounds that can define a space, a character, a moment in the narrative, or even the whole film. They become central to the narrative and often recur over time to punctuate, reinforce, or contradict the narrative or elements within it. These sounds can often also stand as a 'spectacle' in their own right. Voices and music themes can also be part of such sounds (Tom Hanks's voice in *Forrest Gump* is more than just a narrator's voice; it helps define the character). However, most of these sounds are often 'designed' in the sense that they are created by sound designers: their function is never merely literal, but always aimed at achieving the highest level of effectiveness. They can be made of a single recording of a sound, but they are more likely to be the result of a combination of disparate sounds. They can be 'electronically' created, but they are more likely to be recorded from a 'real' source and then modified in a variety of manners. Their effectiveness is clearly dependent on the choices filmmakers make in terms of focus: the greater the drive to highlight individual sounds, the greater the need for 'clarity' in the soundtrack. A film such as *Terminator 2* relies heavily on a few sounds that characterise the whole movie, often by contrast: the liquid metal sound the T2000 makes immediately sets him apart from Schwarzenegger's older terminator model, which still sounds 'mechanical'; the gun the latter employs sounds considerably 'bigger' than any other gun fired in the film; the sound theme that Brad Friedel composed for the movie immediately identifies the film; and Schwarzenegger's accent and delivery are a trademark of the character he plays. It is useful here to point out that sound density is not necessarily dependent on the fact that *Terminator 2* is a sci-fi movie. The huge density of sound at work in most of *Star Wars I: The Phantom Menace*, for example, reduces substantially the possibility of meaningful definition for this is likely to be lost in a mass of sound.

It would be impossible to make even a simple list of examples of definition. For the purpose of this study, it is significant to point out that although this practice is by no means the exclusive domain of contemporary cinema (indeed, many trace the beginning of the art of designing sounds back to *King Kong* and 1930s cinema) this is one of the defining features of sound in the Dolby era. There is a variety of strategies in the way designed sounds can characterise aurally a sequence or a whole movie, and some examples here might help. Films that have a strong central narrative usually employ few designed sounds and repeat them at different points in the movie. *Raging Bull* is a good example of this kind of aural definition: Jake LaMotta's struggle with violence, both in his personal and public life (he is a boxer) is at the core of the film. The most defining sound in the whole movie occurs during the fight sequences. It is an interesting type of designed sound because it is not a single sound but rather a combination of sounds that work as if they were one. Frank Warner's mêlée of animal roars, human breathing, sound of wind and other sounds work over time to give the fight sequences a surreal character. It is a personal world where internal sound, what goes on in the mind of the boxers, is emphasised and contrasted with the wider public watching the boxers, either in person or on television.[25] The sound designed by Warner works all the more effectively because Scorsese films the fighting sequences in an 'intimate' fashion, with frequent close-ups of the boxers and often slowing down the action. In other movies, the film might present the need for sound to aid the creation of a variety of distinctive narrative spaces. In *The Hunt for Red October*, the three submarines at the core of the plot (the 'good' Russian, the 'bad' Russian, and the American) need to be clearly differentiated. This is true of at least three different elements: the ambience of the sub, the sonar 'ping' each of them makes (there is a rather complex interplay between who is 'pinging' whom) and the sound of the torpedoes (again, there are some rather complex moments in the movie). Moreover, the whole movie is based on the fact that the Russian sub, the *Red October*, is supposed to have a new revolutionary propelling system that works ... silently. The sounds that Frank Serafine, Cecelia Hall and George Watters created (it reportedly took six months to come up with the sound of the sub pings alone) provide the necessary definition for all the narrative elements I mentioned.[26]

   Voices can also work to help define a sequence or a whole movie, and can themselves be 'designed'. Films such as *Star Wars* and *Toy Story* have an enormous array of voices, each with its distinctive quality, and all playing as if part of an operatic choir. They occupy different frequencies, have different tone and timbre, their envelope varies from character to character and so on. In other instances, a sound can function like a signature for a specific character: sometimes it is a vocal aspect (Darth Vader's breathing famously defines the character), in other cases it is a sound that plays against expectations (in *Toy Story*, the contrast between the fact that the character of Dino is a tyrannosaurus rex and the 'little' voice he has is used to comic effect). There are times when a sound is or becomes a character, both at an individual level (Indiana Jones's whip, R2D2's bleeping voice) or at a collective level (the submariners in *Das Boot* are defined by the sound of the sonar: when the sonar pings, signalling the possible arrival of depth charges, they cease to be individuals and become one single listening entity).

In creative terms, even the absence of a 'core' sound (a sound that is crucial to the narrative) can function very effectively to define a sequence. In *A Civil Action*, John Travolta's character is a lawyer investigating a series of deaths clustered around a small town as part of a lawsuit against a local firm whose polluting agents are regarded as a possible cause for these deaths. During one of his many trips from the office to the town, he is forced to stop his car on the hard shoulder of a busy highway. Suddenly, the noise of the busy traffic transports his imagination to a similar place where a family, one of the families involved in the lawsuit, is in a car (in a final desperate attempt to rush their child to a hospital). The car is stationary on the hard shoulder: through the rain and amidst the busy traffic rushing by we can see the father and the mother taking turns to try and revive the child, but to no avail. Ordinarily, we would expect to hear much more clearly the sounds of the people inside the car. Instead, we are offered the sound of the busy traffic on this fast road and only occasionally do we hear muffled instances of what goes on in the car. It is the sound of the oncoming rushing traffic that makes the scene, not the sound of the desperate parents. In this sense, the core sound element we expect is 'hidden', replaced by another one whose effectiveness is emphasised by the emotionally poignant effect of the everyday traffic of people going about their business unaware of the tragedy that is taking place.

The combination of the four aspects around which I have structured my analysis of sound is entirely dependent on the specific movie you will look at and listen to (or, to use Chion's expression, 'audioview'). Walter Murch emphasises this particular aspect by suggesting that, for example,

Conceptual density is something that should obey the same rules as loudness dynamics. Your mix, moment by moment, should be as dense (or as loud) as the story and events warrant. A monotonously dense soundtrack is just as wearing as a monotonously loud film. Just as a symphony would be unendurable if all the instruments played together all the time.[27]

Loudness can be a function of contrast (a loud sequence that is preceded and followed by a quiet moment will sound louder than it really is), directionality can help the process of focusing by defusing the density of a particular moment in a movie and hence enhancing the clarity of the sequence by displacing sound to different channels. In other words, to think about sound in the manner I am suggesting is to understand sound as happening over time, as being one of most effective conduits of cinematic movement, and as being as fertile a place for creativity as any aspect of filmmaking can ever aspire to be. In this sense, a brief overview of how sound works in a movie might help emphasise the organic nature of contemporary film sound.

For a more organic approach – part three: no place 'sounds' like home (sound in *Forrest Gump*)

The film's opening sequence, where Forrest is first introduced, is representative of the kind of strong focus that the film employs. Despite being at a bus stop at a relatively large square in the early or mid-afternoon the scene has low sound density in order to emphasise some key sounds that work to define that sequence. Forrest's voice, such an important defining feature in the whole movie, is strongly emphasised by cutting out most extraneous sounds (especially loud sounds – save that of buses, which help to punctuate the passing of time) and backgrounding a few distinguishable 'quiet' elements, such as the chirping of birds and rustling of leaves. This strongly focuses the audience's attention on Forrest's voice. As that sequence becomes one of two key moments to which we keep returning, the choice is all the more important. The other key ambience that works as a benchmark for the movie is actually rather similar in aural characteristics. The Alabama house where Forrest and his mother live is defined by a quiet, almost idyllic ambience. Traffic is never heard (save, once again, for a bus, a school bus this time); the rustling of leaves and the chirping of birds are, again, what shape the soundscape of that place. In this sense, the concept of 'home' in the film functions as a point of contrast between that quiet ambience and the ambience of the places Forrest's 'adventures' take him to: from the roaring crowds of the football field to the battle field of Vietnam and the human mass gathering around the Mall in Washington, DC. It is interesting here to reflect briefly on how camerawork, production design and sound work in relation to each other to create these two key moments we keep returning to. The two locations (i.e. the bus stop and Forrest's home) are very different from each other: most obviously, one is an urban setting and the other a rural home. However, both sound and camerawork work remarkably well to give the two locations a sense of cohesion. The characters at the bus stop are framed rather tightly: we are not offered any wide shots of the whole square, save from the crane shot that opens the movie (the one with the feather drifting down towards Forrest's foot). The 'intimacy' of the framing, especially the way the bench at the bus stop is used as 'focus' for those scenes, encourages audience attention to be given fully to Forrest. In addition to this, the camera often looks head on to Forrest and vice versa. This aids tremendously the work of the sound designer in smoothing the passage from Forrest at the bus stop to Forrest narrating the events, just as it helps bridge the transition back and forth from the bench to the various locations of the story. Indeed, the collaboration between image and sound crew is strongly emphasised by the film's sound designer, Randy Thom:

> Bob [Zemeckis] and Tom Hanks knew that when Forrest was telling his story on the bench he shouldn't be looking at the people he was talking to before or after the flashbacks. The fact that he is looking straight ahead at nothing in particular puts him into the action he is describing and reinforces the idea that what we are hearing is usually his point of view. That opens the door for the sound of the bench to blend a little bit into the beginning of the story he tells, and for the sound associated with those stories to bleed over onto the bench as well. The most obvious example is the helicopters flying over our heads in Vietnam and continuing their fly-by over the city park where Forrest waits for his bus. In moments like that it becomes clear how powerfully picture and sound can work together.[28]

The film's orchestration relies heavily on the interplay between dialogue and music. Although this is true of many movies, in *Forrest Gump* this relationship is particularly complex. The film has an unusual number of songs as well as Tom Hank's voiceover narration to deal with. They both serve the same function, helping audiences trace the passage of time (which could otherwise become a very confusing issue when you consider that Forrest's adventures span from Elvis Presley's early days to the early 1990s). Because of the amount and importance of music and dialogue in the movie, silence and sound effects are used sparsely. However, precisely because of this attention to clarity (there is no wall-to-wall sound in the movie, and great attention is put into maintaining a relatively low density of sound through most scenes) the sounds that help define the different moments in Forrest's life and events he goes through are even more emphasised. The film's narrative traces historical development by portraying both events in which Forrest plays a key role and other moments where Forrest is simply another bystander or witness. Examples of the former are the Vietnam war, the peace gathering in Washington, and Forrest's sport exploits both as a football player and as a ping pong player; examples of the latter are the assassination attempts of political figures (George Wallace, John Ford and Ronald Reagan, but also John and Bobby Kennedy, John Lennon), and the moon landing. All of these moments in Forrest's life are defined clearly by the way 'designed sounds' characterise them. In the case where Forrest is only marginally involved, television pictures are used as a device to 'cover' those events. However, sound is often more intrusive than the image in these instances and helps punctuate those points more forcefully. In particular, the gun shots of all the assassination attempts are very much in the foreground and can be distinctively heard (not just casually 'overheard'), and Neil Armstrong's 'One small step for man, one huge leap for mankind' speech is clearly heard even though the television screen showing the event is rather small and the camera moves away from it.

The best examples of how those individually designed sounds help define sequences come when we look at the events in the narrative where Forrest is personally involved. Each 'moment' in Forrest's life is emphasised by a few carefully designed sounds. The leg braces in his young days (the sound of Forrest breaking loose of the braces is particularly emphasised as it is the beginning of a new stage in his life), the football crowds in his college years, the rain (there is markedly evident variety in the way the rain sounds in the different moments of the movie) and helicopters in Forrest's tour of duty in Vietnam (the solo sound of a helicopter reminds us where we are when there is a cut from the bus station to Forrest in an army hospital), the sound of ping pong (all rather different from each other according to the 'kind' of ping pong that he plays: solo, one bat, two bats, and so on), the seagulls in his shrimping boat captain days, the music tracks in the running sequence (there are five different songs in that sequence alone), and, most importantly perhaps, the moments of quietness that define Forrest's times with both his mother and with Jenny at the house in Alabama. All these sounds are to be expected and are hardly new (helicopters and Vietnam are a rather well-trodden path in Hollywood movies!), but the way they are used in the movie suggests the strategy that I outlined before and the kind of control over material that Thom and his sound crew strive for. In this sense, it is useful to remember what this soundtrack is not, and could just as easily have been. It is not very dense, despite obvious potential for density (Vietnam, huge crowd gatherings, assassinations, etc.). It does not use surround sound very often: music and a few effects, especially in the Vietnam ambush sequence, are most of what is there. This is a strong indication of the sound strategy employed in the movie: since Forrest's voice is what drives the narrative, and density is low, to begin using surround sound more frequently would have meant 'complicating' the soundtrack for the sake of complication. Interestingly, Thom is unequivocal about the fact that this was a conscious, joint decision on his part and the director's early on in the process:

> Surrounds were an interesting issue on *Gump*. What with Pro Logic and AC3 there has been a flood of interest in surrounds, and the tendency now is sometimes to put lots of stuff into the surrounds just for the sake of novelty. Some movies can benefit from heavy use of surrounds and some will suffer from it. Bob Zemeckis and I agreed that *Gump* was in the latter category, so we used surrounds sparingly. Most of the score was bled into the surrounds, some ambiences, a couple of aircraft flyovers, some bullet-by's, and that's about it. I'm not against surrounds, but we thought there was a danger of distracting the audience from this particular story by feeding too much material into the rear of the theatre.[29]

The consequence of all the creative choices I have outlined is a film whose soundtrack can be described as heavy on contrast, with a simple orchestration, strong focus and a marked degree of definition. The adjectives I am using, heavy, simple, strong and marked, are not intended to be evaluative of the 'quality' of the soundtrack. Nor is there 'one right way' of doing sound for *Forrest Gump*. It is not too difficult to envisage ways in which less emphasis could have been placed on Tom Hanks's voiceover, where density could have been much higher, and consequently with a much more complex level of orchestration required. However, the ways in which these different choices would have affected the narrative should act less as a value judgement on the filmmakers' choice and more as another reminder how central a role sound plays in filmmaking.

Notes

1   To name but one famous example: despite the original aim of Truffaut and other French filmmakers/critics, it would be difficult to imagine auteurism today without the use of some form of textual analysis.

2   A very useful collection of different terminologies of sound provided by some of these scholars can be found online at www.filmsound.org /terminology.htm (accessed 10 October 2003).

3   Chion 1994, pp. 185–213.

4   *Ibid.*, p. 188.

5   G. Sergi, 'The Hollywood Sonic Playground: The Spectator as Listener', in Richard Maltby and Melvyn Stokes (eds.), *Hollywood Spectatorship* (London: British Film Institute, 2001), pp. 121–131.

6   Although early signs of an impending sound revolution were noticeable in the early and mid-1970s, it did not become apparent to the general public until the late 1970s with the success of films such as *Star Wars*, *Close Encounters of the Third Kind*, and *Apocalypse Now*.

7   Walter Murch, 'Dense Clarity, Clear Density', available at: www.ps1. org/cut/volume/murch.html (accessed 1 September 2002).

8   This should not be taken to be a 'mark of expertise' separating those who know about sound from those who do not. Despite listening to the movie several times in preparation for a conference and a book, I had never noticed this effect until the supervising sound editor of the movie, Larry Blake, pointed it out in a presentation at a conference on sound.

9   I do not wish to discount the inevitable problems inherent to talking to Hollywood practitioners. Nor do I wish to exclude my own work as I have often relied heavily on theoretical arguments in my writing. However, today's means of communication mean that it is no longer necessary to jump on a plane and travel thousands of miles to ask a few questions: email and telephone exchanges can prove just as fruitful.

10 It is important to remember that a good post-production sound facility in Hollywood can cost upwards of $1,000 per hour, thus time *is* money in sound terms as much as it is for any other aspect of film production.

11 To quote but one example, Gary Rydstrom in 2002 followed work on movies such as *Star Wars – Attack of the Clones* and *Minority Report* with designing sound for *Amandla! A Revolution in Four Part Harmony*, a documentary about the role of music in South Africa during apartheid.

12 For a good example, see Rick Altman, '24-Track Narrative? Robert Altman's *Nashville*' *Cinema* (Vol. 5, Issue 1.3, 1991).

13 See my interview with Gary Rydstrom on page 163.

14 Weis later wrote a book on sound in Hitchcock's movies: *The Silent Scream – Alfred Hitchcock's Soundtrack* (Rutherford Fairleigh: Dickinson University Press, 1982).

15 Elisabeth Weis, 'The Sound of One Wing Flapping', *Film Comment* (Vol. 14, Issue 5, 1978), pp. 42–48.

16 See the Directors Guild of America web site at www.dga.org (accessed 1 September 2002).

17 Forum discussion with Randy Thom, available online at www.filmsound.org/casforum.htm (accessed 23 January 2004).

18 I accept the view that both sound and image are 'photographed', but I believe it is more important to focus on the conceptual dimension at this stage. For an excellent discussion of this ontological problem see Tom Levin's 'The Acoustic Dimension', *Screen* (Vol. 25, Issue 3, May/June 1984), pp. 55–68.

19 I should specify here that silence, as a filmic term, is not too dissimilar from the concept of silence in real life. When I use the word silence, I do not mean complete absence of sound (nigh impossible to achieve in any case), but rather a minimal presence of sound: for example a mountain top on a clear day will be devoid of everyday sounds, especially loud sounds. Despite some low-level sounds, such as a gentle breeze or a distant rustling of leaves, most of us would identify that as 'silence'.

20 The most famous account on this is Michel Chion's *The Voice in the Cinema* (New York: Columbia University Press, 1999).

21 Robert Bresson, quoted in Belton and Weis (eds.) 1985, p. 149.

22 Walter Murch provides us with the most effective definition of 'layer' when he says: 'Let's define a layer as a conceptually-unified series of sounds which run more or less continuously, without any large gaps between individual sounds. A single seagull cry, for instance, does not make a layer'. Extract from Murch, 'Dense Clarity, Clear Density'.

23 *Ibid.*

24 Extract from Christopher Cook, *Dancing Shadows*, a BBC Radio 4 production (2000), part 3 of 4.

25 The other relevant designed sound in the fight sequences, the photographers' flash, works to highlight this contrast between private and public.

26 For more see Frank Serafine, 'Creating the Undersea Sounds of Red October', *American Cinematographer* (Vol. 71, Issue 9, September 1990), pp. 67–72.

27 Murch, 'Dense Clarity, Clear Density'.

28 Randy Thom, 'Mixing A Different Box of Chocolates – A Few Notes on Forrest Gump', available at www.filmsound.org/randythom/forrest.htm (accessed 20 September 2002).

29 *Ibid.*

3

Interviews with the makers of sound: Gary Rydstrom

Gary Rydstrom is a multiple Oscar winner for films such as *Titanic*, *Saving Private Ryan*, *Terminator 2* and *Jurassic Park*. He has collaborated with some of the most influential directors in Hollywood, from Steven Spielberg to James Cameron and Paul Thomas Anderson. He is also Director of Creative Operations at Skywalker Sound, a division of Lucasfilm, and has provided the inspiration for Dolby Laboratories' latest sound system, Dolby EX.[1] More significantly, Rydstrom is one of the most articulate professionals in Hollywood today, and his comments are both incisive and revealing of the creative process involved in creating film sound. The following interview is the result of an ongoing dialogue carried out over the past few years through meetings, interviews and emailing.

Gianluca Sergi: I'd like to start by asking a asking you a very basic question to which we can hopefully get a straight answer: what is sound design?

Gary Rydstrom: Well sound design is a bit of a confusing term and I use it because I come out of a tradition in Northern California, especially in terms of what Walter Murch did, what Ben Burtt was doing. They used the term to mean someone who was really the architect of the soundtrack from the earliest point in the film all the way through the mix so it was really the equivalent of an art director, someone who thought of the whole soundtrack and how it was going to come together to give it a consistency. Within that there is this idea of creating sound effects, which I also like to do, to create a library and 'manufacture' sound effects but I think it's much bigger than that. It's really trying to be the person that the director can turn to for the whole soundtrack and make sure that it comes together appropriately for the film.

Sergi: Before we get into the specifics of that can you give us an idea of how you get involved in a project?

Rydstrom: First of all, I get a phone call to see whether I'm interested in a film that's many years away, or maybe it hasn't been shot yet. I get that first phone call and, these days, what's nice is that I get projects usually from people that I worked with before. So, it comes down to that first offer, that first phone call. Part of the trick of doing this job is to wonder if a film is going to be good or interesting long before that film is shot so you are taking a bit of a risk like anybody else.

Sergi: Let's say you are on board a project, what happens next?

Rydstrom: Hopefully there'll be a script and the first thing that I do, because usually I'm on before anybody else starts, is just to think about the feel of the film. The most important job early on for someone doing sound design is to figure out the personality of the film, what kind of soundtrack will fit the mood and the personality of that film. Each film really has its own distinct feeling to it and so you start thinking in terms of what that feeling is going to be and what you can do with the soundtrack that will help it. What I like about sound is that there is no blank page really; it's not like writing and it's not even like visual effects when you create something out of nothing: you go to the computer and create a dinosaur out of the computer, out of nothing. What I like about sound is that the first step for me is going out into the world and recording real-life things, recording props, animals, whatever, and it's like nature photography for me, so it's a way to come up with ideas just through the random interacting with the world. So that first step really is to come up with those ideas: where should we go to start recording sound effects, what would be the most promising places to find things to record. Then on the way it's a discovery process: the thing that I thought was cool, it's not so cool, but this thing down the road is really cool. You start collecting raw sounds from the world and then those raw sounds become the building blocks with what you come back to the studio and create.

It's important when creating sound effects, when creating a soundtrack, to have the control that comes from building up from little bits and pieces so you do end up with hundreds and hundreds of little titbits of sound. The job back in the studio is almost like panning for gold; you are sifting through all this stuff and you are looking for those interesting moments, those things that you captured when recording sounds for your library.

It then becomes a big puzzle in my mind: I'm starting to think about these sounds here that seem to group into what'll be a great vehicle sound, these will be great ambiences, this is a good feel for a creature, these will make great doors. You start grouping them and experimenting and throwing a lot of stuff out. The way I work, I use a synclavier to fairly quickly take samples of different sounds and layer them on top of each other and see what I can turn them into. Part of that jigsaw puzzle is saying: the ambience for this location should not only be good for the location itself but it should be a great contrast in the context of the movie to this other location, which will have maybe a higher frequency sound; in this location I want a lower frequency sound; in this vehicle I want to be low and smooth, in this vehicle I want to be high and rough so you start orchestrating the various sounds in the soundtrack, how they are going to work in context with each other. The whole key to sound is context; sounds are always playing in relation to what came before and what came after so when you start creating a library of sounds for a movie is very important to consider the whole thing. I've heard people talking about it in the past: 'always save the biggest gun for the hero' kind of idea so you have various guns but you want to have a bad guy gun that sounds very different than the hero gun, the Indiana Jones gun sounds different from the bad guy gun. So you think in terms of the whole picture in coming up with these sounds.

Sergi: You used the word 'orchestration' and that's an interesting concept because it suggests that you have an overall idea of what the picture ought to sound like. Is that what it is, or is it my interpretation?

Rydstrom: No, that's exactly what it is. Sound happens over time. What makes sound different than the visual is that you can take a visual cue and you can take a picture and fairly instantly 'read it'.

Sound is always about time, even what you think of as the short-est sound; everything is happening over time. It's all the same ele-ments that make music music. There is nothing different in what the building blocks of music are to what the building blocks of the soundtrack in a movie are: it's all pitch, and rhythm and orches-tration of various elements happening over time, that's all there is. I wish I knew how to orchestrate music literally, because I'm not that good musically but I think that that would be the best way of thinking about putting together a soundtrack. It really is orchestration so when you are thinking about what sounds go well together, what instruments would play well together either in concert or in contrast and how you build the music to climax at various points and then to rest so everything is shaped over time and the same thing with the soundtrack, you are always thinking in terms of time and layers. People ask after a movie is done, espe-cially a big movie, how many thousands of sounds were going on at any one time. The truth is that you shouldn't have thousands of sounds going on at any one time; you can have thousands of sounds over time, but the complexity for a soundtrack is sequen-tial – it happens over time. It's not hitting you all at once: now I'm hearing this element of the soundtrack, and now that one; it evolves and changes over time.

Sergi: Presumably, at some point or other, you come to realise that there are certain sounds that are perhaps more important than others in the movie and that deserve a little more attention. They might be signature sounds, for example, or sounds that are repeated over time and that are particularly important for the narrative. Can you give us some example of that?

Rydstrom: Sure. Any movie is going to have sounds that should be fairly unique or completely unique to it. The obvious example is *Jurassic Park* because you knew that the sound of the dinosaurs was going to be the signature sound of the movie; so you know where to put your effort, where to concentrate. Those are the sounds that are going to make that movie sound unique. In every movie you need to decide what to focus on early on to make it interesting. In *Saving Private Ryan* there was obvious weaponry and things that we needed to find the real sounds for, but we also knew that the way the film was shot had made such a point of view, especially the first battle, that the sounds we needed to focus on getting were what battle sounds like from on the ground, from the soldiers' point of view, bullets pass-bys and whiz-bys the head and impacts and just the cacophony of battle from the point of view of a lone soldier on the ground in the middle of that sound as opposed to a big, all-encompassing sound of battle.

Sergi: Many people have commented in the past, including yourself, about the fact that when you are thinking about a sound that can be used in a particular moment in a film, it is not the literal quality of that sound, in other words it is not the sound that the object on the screen would make in real life, but the effectiveness in narrative terms of that sound that you are going for. Is that the way you work?

Rydstrom: Absolutely. I think what we are doing all the time when we are cutting sound in a movie is making note of our own emotional reaction to a sound, so even the simplest sound like a door creak or a cricket chirp you choose because of your emotional reaction to it, and I've always been less interested generally in being realistic than in being dramatic. There are certainly times when you want to be true to the real sound of a car, the real sound of a gun, but very often in movie sound you want to create the effect, the feeling of it, and it's amazing how many times something will sound 'right' because you artificially created something that had the right feeling than if you had done the literal thing. You know, we are not making documentaries. If you are making documentaries about the actual sound it is different, but in movie sound very often you are just trying to make the audience experience the correct feeling for anything from a gun shot to just a spooky forest ambience. You want it to be realistic emotionally and dramatically as opposed to in reality. The old story in Hollywood is that if you record a gun, a real gun and put it into a movie, into a *Terminator*-type movie, it'll never seem big enough, so you sweeten it with cannon blasts and canyon echoes and all sort of other things to make it movie reality. If you think about it, the images are blown much bigger than in reality on a huge screen. It's all very subjective, and it's about finding the right feeling. One of the great moments of pride I had was after we did *Saving Private Ryan*, in which we did take a fairly literal approach to some of the sounds of the machine guns and the artillery of that war and tried to stay true to it, but there were other times when we couldn't, or I wanted to find the sound that seemed emotionally correct. There was a scene in that movie where these German tanks come into a town, and they keep coming, and they are coming for five minutes. You hear them off in the distance and they (the soldiers) are preparing for battle while you hear these tanks echoing through the buildings, slowly coming closer, and closer, and closer. Afterwards I heard from several veterans, people who'd been in tank battles, that it was nice to hear that distinctive sound of tanks approaching captured so well in a movie, and that was one of the sounds in the movie that was artificially created: I just scraped things on concrete to get the squealing of the tank threads and I made rhythms not from real tanks motors but from other motors and then I artificially created these pulsing rhythms and did it artificially in that case, but emotionally it worked for the people who should know, so I was happy about that.

Sergi: You mentioned a couple of times the word 'subjective'. Tom Holman [inventor of the THX sound system and former chief engineer at Skywalker Sound] once told me in an interview that sometimes that particular drive that a sound designer almost naturally has of going out looking for the most effective sound rather than the more literal one might create problems with directors.[2] For example, when you do the final mix, when you lock picture and sound, simply because a director might not be prepared to hear that particular sound at that moment, he might be shocked by it. We are talking about 'politics' in many ways. Has that ever happened to you?

Rydstrom: Yeah. I did a movie called *Single White Female* with Barbet Schroeder and it took place in New York, in an apartment building. Early on he had talked about wanting to use the world around us in the apartment building, the world of cab drivers and traffic and creaky buildings and plumbing to create a psychological soundtrack as opposed to being more realistic. So I did some sounds I thought were purely subjective, purely emotional, rhythmic, very 'David Lynch–Alan Splet' like sounds, since he was willing to go that way. When he heard them he said 'Rydstrom, what you have done with these sounds, it is fantastic' and I said 'Oh, thank you very much' and then he said 'I think maybe it is too fantastic' [laughs], so that was his way of saying let's go back to reality a little bit. I just did *Minority Report* with Spielberg and there is a scene where the Tom Cruise character is drugged by this back-alley surgeon and it's a very eerie, scary, bizarre scene so I put in these sounds that weren't related to anything at all, they weren't the reality of what was going on. Spielberg wanted to know what they were and he kept asking me 'What is it?' and I had to finally say 'Well, I would say it's ... plumbing, I don't know, plumbing'. Then he kept referring to it and he'd say 'There I'd like the plumbing, there I would like to take out the plumbing'. It is very subjective both in the way an audience perceives it and also in how you work with a director, what you buy as the proper sound effect at that moment and also what the director is going to buy as well, so it's always a negotiation really between the two of you.

Sergi: As you say, there is a certain amount of 'negotiation' going on there.

Rydstrom: Sure and I have to say, and I don't want to appear somewhat negative, but I wish that in general filmmakers were more open to using sound in a less realistic way. I think that everybody in the film industry, including sound people, sometimes restrict themselves to being more literal than they should. Some of the best filmmaking has treated sound less literally and it's shown itself to be very effective. But it is considered risky in a way that I don't think it should be. I think it is one of the fights that I wish we didn't lose this much because there is more potential in the soundtrack than most films make use of.

Sergi: What you've just touched on, the issue of being more conservative, shall we use that word, in terms of choices when it comes to the soundtrack is quite striking. You find, repeatedly, that people will say 'There are certain things you should never do' or 'There are certain things that I would never do'. For example, one of the best examples is the dialogue. One of the key tenets is that the dialogue stays up front, where the screen is, where the action is, and that you very rarely move it to the surround channel, to the back of the auditorium. I know there are some technical reasons for that but I suspect that it is an issue of not wanting to 'push it'. What's your take on that?

Rydstrom: It's dangerous to have rules. There are things that work, but there are also things that are too restrictive and you end up making everything the same. If you think about the rules too much all the films start seeming the same and all the films' soundtracks start seeming the same. I think it's very important to, I guess, break the rules but more to the point you really need to think about what's good for the movie at any given moment and it might be that you need to say 'To hell with the rules' it's just the movie telling you what to do, the movie saying 'I want to move the dialogue in the surround' because, say, in the movie *Strange Days*, which is about a point of view of someone captured on this futuristic technology that can capture experience, and so part of the experience of life is that things happen around us, including dialogue, so the movie is saying 'let's put the dialogue behind us'. I think rules are less important then looking at each film individually and saying what's going to be the most important thing. What I find happens when people think about sound, including sound people, is that they think that the dialogue is the literal part of the track – you get the information from dialogue – and then you have music at the other end of the spectrum that is pure emotion and that is really not connected to anything, and a lot of soundtracks have dialogue and music and really don't make use of this vast area in between that is what the rest of the track can be, which is some combination of literal and figurative sound that can always be doing something to set mood and to get you inside a character head and to be dramatic.

A lot of approaches say that sound should be this: 'If I see something on the screen put a sound there so the audience believe it's really happening' and that's the extent of it. But even the simplest choice in sound, the cricket chirp, can be made from a dramatic point of view so that the pace of the cricket chirp is appropriate to the mood of the scene. I'm much more interested to pick a cricket chirp even if it's from Australia for a movie that takes place in Ohio that is appropriate to the drama of that scene; if that's what works, that's what works. I think there's a thinking that sound is fairly obvious: you see something you put a sound in and you are done, as opposed of making use of this whole 'angle' on the film to do all sorts of wonderful things to support the film itself. To me what makes it all more powerful is that you have two levels of a film: you have the visual side that is giving you some information and you have the sound side. They are really two aspects to the film and they are equally important and equally able to convey information.

What I think is most powerful in films is when they are giving you two different levels of information. In *Das Boot* there is a scene when they are diving deeper and deeper in the submarine and the pressure is building up until eventually the bolts pop and they are hoping not to be discovered by a ship going overhead. That scene is very tense because it stays on close-ups of the characters as they are nervously, silently waiting to get through this. Meanwhile you hear the creaks of the sub, and you hear the ships going overhead, you hear all this off-screen world that tells you that part of the narrative where the visuals can tell you the human part and they can get you close to the faces so the image and the sound are telling you the story from two different angles. Very often in movies people give you the same information from sound as they are giving you from the visuals as opposed to two different 'angles' on it. In the war film I did, *Saving Private Ryan*, we did the same thing. The visuals were very close up and the way Spielberg shot, especially the opening battle, was very 'close' and confusing visually. You didn't get the wide scope of battle. You didn't see the Germans on one hand and the allies coming up the beaches on the other side and you got this big establishing shot of the battle. It was always shot from a very intimate angle and the soundtrack's job was to tell you the story that is going on all around us. It was an effective use for the track to tell parts of the story that we were not seeing, and vice-versa. That's what makes much more powerful cinema to me than being literal and single-minded about it.

Sergi: That introduces another topic I wanted to talk about with you, and again it refers to these aesthetic rules that are passed down 'from generation to generation'. One of these rules seems to be that you should never distract the audience from what is happening on the screen. Many sound people, and directors, often refer to this as 'key rule number one'. In other words, the worry there is that if you put sound in the surround, that is, sound that you are not seeing on screen, your audience might feel distracted by the sound happening in the back of the theatre and be taken out of the narrative. What's your take on that?

Rydstrom: There are certainly cases like that. If you put for no good reason the sound of a door opening into the surrounds that might make people turn around and think 'Somebody is coming into the theatre', or another is when you put a phone ringing in the back. There are things that you can do that are just lame and that might take an audience out of a movie, but my strong feeling about it is that since we are predators, the way we perceive the world is that we see up front, we see up front very well, and we hear all around us. We hear 360°, we are always hearing 360° so why shouldn't movies reflect that reality when it's dramatically appropriate? I don't think audiences will be distracted, if you design the soundtrack properly, by a world that is going on behind them and off-screen. In fact, that's where some of the greatest potential for a soundtrack comes from because as I said the soundtrack can very often tell part of the story that is not being told visually so that off-screen world, so called, which includes things that you can out in the surround can be very effective for giving a sense of location, which can also give us a sense of mood and that it reminds us that there might be two people talking but there's a car hurtling toward them on the freeway that's coming from behind us. It tells us a story that's important without being distracting. I think we are able to get through life by looking straight in front of us and listening all around, that's the way we take in the world, so there is no reason why movies should not reflect that same reality.

Sergi: What is re-recording mixing, and what do you do as a re-recording mixer?

Rydstrom: On my door I used to have my title as 'Re-re-re-re-recording mixer' [laughs]. It refers to taking things that have been recorded once and putting them back to a console and recording them again. This is to distinguish it from someone who's on a scoring stage mixing live music on to tape. So re-recording mixing is taking material that has been edited – sound effects, dialogue, music, foley – and starting to funnel all those elements to the final mix of the movie. It starts with pre-mixing when we'll take different elements from the sound effects and dialogue, foley and the music separately – get those under control and start making some early decisions about how sounds are working together, and how they move across the screen, and equalisation and all the things that you can do on a mixing board. Then the pre-mixing moves to final mixing when now we are choosing how to layer all these many different elements that are available on the soundtrack. Whereas editing is a process of putting things in, placing things in synch to the film, the mixing part, I find, is usually a process of taking away. So we prepare too much, everyone always prepare too much, for the soundtrack: you can't play it all together, you can't take it all in, it gets too cacophonous, too confusing, so the mixing process most importantly is about, again, focusing the audience attention on what's important at any given time. If the music is carrying a scene you play up the music, you balance it in and out with the dialogue and sound effects. You know, it's like three or four different roller coasters, everyone is moving up and down, heading off to another element that then has its moment and then heads off to another element. It's a dance really between the different elements that are available on a soundtrack and how you play them, which is something that I guess works so subliminally that you don't realise that the effectiveness of a simple choice of level and how dramatically different it can be.

How you play music and dialogue and sound effects moment to moment really affects the effectiveness of a scene, the drama of a scene, so I think it's probably misunderstood by a lot of people as being a fairly technical exercise of just getting everything at the right level and you're done but it comes down to a constant choice being made over what elements to hear, how much of them to hear. This is where the 'sound over time' issue becomes important because you are thinking about the shape of a scene, the shape of a reel, the shape of a whole movie so that things have this up and down, peaks and valleys.

Sergi: You mentioned the issue of choosing what goes in the background and what stays in the foreground and that sounds like one of the most creative aspects of what you make decisions about. You have all these hundreds of different sounds and there is a process of selection that needs to go on. Can you tell us more about that? First of all, who's present when you do the final mix?

Rydstrom: We just did the latest *Star Wars* film, Episode II, and we had three mixers. I mixed the sound effects and foley, then we had a mixer for the dialogue and one for the music. So there's three of us working together, and it's really like driving a car with three different steering wheels so we are trying to work together, and it really is like dancing. Then there is the director: often he is not there for the minute-by-minute part, but the director is involved because they are the final arbiter of what works, and the thing is that there are choices all the time that you have to make and things that go on to the equivalent of the 'cutting room floor', we need a term like the 'mixing room floor', because a lot of things are left on the mixing room floor. Those choices about what works best for the movie aren't always obvious and the director is who makes that final decision. One of the bigger conflicts that happen in the mix, the most obvious one, is sound effects and music. The dialogue usually, unless it's considered ambience, has to be heard – we make sure that audiences understand it – but then there is this conflict between sound effects and music partly because they are both tonal, they both have rhythms, they both eat up the track. If you put a type of sound with a certain type of music you might not have clarity in the music, or the music might eat up the clarity of the sound effect and that relationship is what we spend a lot of the time working out in the final mix. It's really orchestrating through the console: it's orchestrating by choosing which elements are going to work best together.

Sergi: Is it a fair thing to say that there isn't that much collaboration between the composer and the people who work on the sound-track?

Rydstrom: It's very fair to say. There are occasional movies where people are lucky enough to have a true collaboration, but in reality what often happens is that the composer is doing their work up until the last minute. They have a fairly big job to do and it doesn't show up on our doorstep until the final mix begins. So very often we haven't heard the music, we haven't played it with everything else until we are in the final mix trying to make it all work. That's just a matter of scheduling, and time and reality. There can be discussions early on, and at the very least I try to go to music spotting sessions to be there and talk and think of things with the composer in terms of, most importantly, what scenes the music is going to 'take', because the music doesn't *have* to be there; sound effects, to some extent, are there all the time, but the music can come and go, and where you choose to start it and where you choose to stop it is a very important element of how effective the music is going to be. And since it is orchestration, now we are talking 'über-orchestration'! We are talking about orchestration between the music, which is complex in itself, and the rest of the track that has to play with it and so, if we are good, we'll have early discussions about the type of instrumentation, the frequencies the composer is thinking about, and the frequencies the sound effects are more likely going to take. I was lucky enough when we did *Jurassic Park* because John Williams composed the music here at Skywalker Ranch so I was able to play him some of the dinosaur vocals that I had created early on. He thought of them in terms of the pitch, so he would say 'That dinosaur is a cello, this dinosaur feels more like flutes' and then he was able to think about in terms of writing the music and orchestrating it for those scenes. This is pretty rare, but it works well when it happens.

Sergi: Is it also true that the composer is very rarely present during the final mix, when those kinds of decisions are made?

Rydstrom: In my experience the composer is very rarely in the final. They are usually working on the next film [laughs], but it is very useful [to have them there]. I have done the last couple of Spielberg movies where John Williams took a very strong interest on how things were working, not to just 'protect' his music but to make sure that it was all working for the film so in *AI* and *Minority Report* he would come by for at least playbacks of reels as we were working on them and he was able to see how his music was working so that he could change cues, change the way the music was edited and come up with ideas, and that was invaluable. I like it when the composer can have the time to come to the final mix, as long as they are not there just to … well, you don't want to do this, but sometimes you feel like you are there to 'protect' your work which is not really important. You should be there to see how it is all coming together and see what you can do to make it better. I think one of the areas that can most improve in making a soundtrack is for the sound effects department and the music department to work better together, because that relationship between sound effects and music is such an important one for the mix.

Sergi: The accepted wisdom is that the director has creative control over just about anything but, although obviously the director has ultimate say as to what goes and what doesn't, you are actually painting a picture where the sound people, especially in the final mix, have quite a lot of latitude in terms of creative input. Is that a fair way of describing it?

Rydstrom: Yeah, I think different directors have different amounts of 'hands-on' but in general you can say that the whole idea of making the movie and making the soundtrack is so complex, by virtue of what it is, that a director is not able to create everything that comes into the final product. For me in the mix the director's job most importantly is to be at that point, funny enough, the most objective observer of the mix of that movie to see what's working and make sure that we are helping the movie, not hurting it. Film directors are dependent upon a fairly large group of creative talents who for a good part of the time are working alone. The auteur theory and that whole concept I think sometimes ignores the fact that movies are too complex for any one person to create everything themselves. Their job is to make the paradigm that the movie exist in and to be the final 'say' about what works and what doesn't work but, man, there are many people who do a lot of work, including the sound people, that affects the overall movie, whether it works.

Sergi: You once told me, speaking about *Terminator 2* and working with James Cameron, that he often works by taking sounds out, in other words using a 'less is more' approach. That's interesting especially because Cameron has been described, especially after *Titanic*, as a director of 'excesses', the richness and wealth of detail, and so on, especially in the images. Have I understood you correctly? Do you believe that Cameron has a different approach to sound than he has to images?

Rydstrom: He has a very distinctive approach to sound that is based a lot on contrast. It's really true, he does believe that less is more, and I think you can make an argument for it visually as well. The counterintuitive result of it from the soundtrack point of view, which is really fascinating to me, and I really learned this from *Terminator 2* and I learned it from him, is that people thought when *Terminator 2* came out 'My God, it's huge! It has some of the densest, biggest action stuff we've ever seen'. Cameron's trick to making it seem big and dense is to keep it focused, and I think he does that visually as well as sound wise. On the soundtrack he really didn't want to have a lot of extraneous sound; he wanted to focus moment to moment on 'and now we are in the front of the engine of the truck and we hear that, now we are not and don't hear the truck at all; now we hear this, we hear the motorcycle' and so on. He was very focused on what sounds happened when and by virtue of taking out, which is always what we do in mixing, but he sometimes took it to extremes, things that weren't necessary, since you are not being literal about it, you just take out background and other things that are not so important, it made each of the things that we left seem bigger. Even in the action scenes in that movie less was more – the more paired down the track became, each of the moments had more freedom to live: the explosions seemed bigger, the big climactic moments seemed bigger.

Sergi: Let's move on to what could feasibly be described as the opposite of this approach. You mentioned before the opening sequence of *Saving Private Ryan*. In many ways that's the kind of sequence that wins you an Oscar: it's the perfect example of complexity. Can you tell us about how do you go about organising a scene that immediately is huge?

Rydstrom: If sound effects editing is knitting, that scene was knitting a very huge piece of clothing [laughs]. That was perhaps the most detailed sound work I've ever been involved with. The trick with that scene was to try to express the chaos of what war sounds like but also to articulate it. That whole track was built up from the smallest little pieces: each bullet impact was cut in individually, and each bullet pass-by and guns. It was built up from the tiniest detail and orchestrated. The first thing that made that scene effective was two choices that Spielberg made. One was the way he shot it: he didn't spend a lot of time establishing the literalness of what was happening. He was very subjective in the way his hand-held camera work was done, so you took to the scene as though you were this unnamed soldier experiencing the landing in Normandy. Because it looked subjective, it opened up the possibility of playing that scene as though you are experiencing it as an audience member. The other choice he made that was really important to me was to leave the music out and have no John Williams' score until the battle was over. In fact, none of the battles in that movie had traditional score. The score was always used to react to something horrific that we had just been through, as a lightning rod for our emotions after we had gone through twenty minutes of horrific warfare, then you stop and the music would come on and be a life saver; it would be something that you could grab on to and your emotions could drain into it as a reaction. Spielberg was very smart to know that having the score, any kind of score, the greatest score in the world, over those battle scenes would take away the subjective feeling of it; you would no longer feel like you were there, you would feel like you were watching a movie. By making that choice then he opened up the track to what we could do with the sound effects by both making it realistic and making it dramatic.

Spielberg, like Cameron, also knows the importance of contrast: he built into the scene 'hooks' that we could use to give a scene, that could have been unrelenting, moments of contrast. This is an important thing for directors: the great directors, like Spielberg, think about sound and that aspect of their film from the beginning, as they plan the shoot, not after the shooting is done and the editing is done. So in that opening scene he came up with the idea of, in one case, of camera perspective where the camera goes above and below water. As we go above water, we have the full sound of battle, and when we go under water we are momentarily cocooned from it, the battle gets muffled and goes away. The other idea that he had that way was the Tom Hanks character would be shell-shocked and lose hearing. We would go into a point of view, into the Tom Hanks character, and the natural sounds of the battle would drop away. We were left with what I tried to make into a sort of listening to a sea-shell kind of roar, all the realistic sounds drifted away, dropped away, and it gave us a another point of view on battle. So now we are seeing images without having the realistic sounds go with them and that becomes a different take on it. We can see a man carrying his arm but we are not hearing the reality of it, and we take that in very differently than we were earlier on. He was shifting the perspective that way and making use of these stylistic techniques to offer us the possibility for contrast in the sound, which was really brilliant.

Sergi: We've talked about all the creative aspects involved in your job, but there still seems to be an understanding amongst people that sound is a technical part of filmmaking, rather than a more creative, artistic part. In other words, the afterthought to the image, the second fiddle, or whatever other routinely employed expression you want to use. What would you say to that view?

Rydstrom: One of the reasons why I love film is because it's a perfect blend, a 50/50 blend of art and technology. Every aspect of films: a great cinematographer is equally well versed in the creative use of images and the technical part of using a camera and lighting. Acting is both technical and creative, and certainly a director in a movie has to know what the technical abilities are throughout the making of a movie, as well as having creative goals for the movie itself. Movies became a great reflection of the twentieth century because they so neatly followed along that century in both how technology advanced and art advanced. Movies were the most important art form of the twentieth century because they were very heavily technical, and dependent on technology for their very existence, as well as creative. Every part of filmmaking is both artistic and technical and it's a little insulting when parts of filmmaking, like sound, are considered more technical than artistic, or sometimes all technical. This is something we fight against when it comes down to credits, which is indicative of this. The Directors Guild of America, which control how credits are given out in movies in this country, consider any sound credit to be a technical credit: that is, it's not allowed to be a head credit in a movie the way, say, a costume designer and other people have. They have deemed the sound world of filmmaking to be strictly technical, as if it was negative cutting. Of course, it isn't, and the best filmmakers know it isn't and make use of it. The danger is that, if you think something is just technical you are ignoring the artistic capabilities of it, and so directors do it at their peril if they think that it is a technical exercise. Sound people themselves, I think, suffer from the idea that it is simpler than it really is, than there isn't great potential for creative use of the soundtrack. And if we buy into the fact that other people think that it's a technical exercise then we are just hurting the movie in the long run and hurting film as an art form because it is true that half of the experience for the audience is coming from sound and if you don't use it to its full capacity you are not using film to its full capacity.

Notes

1 For more on Skywalker Sound see www.skysound.com (accessed 1 March 2003).

2 In a conversation I had with Tom Holman in July 1998 he stated that 'Some sound designers tell me that when you are putting up music, everybody expects that, when you are putting up dialogue, everybody expects that, when you are putting up the kind of sound effect that is sort of "see a car, hear a car", the literal sound effect, they expect that too. They expect the ambience of a space. However, as soon as you do something different from that then people start noticing and wondering what are you up to, start getting concerned or difficult, or in some cases interested'.

4

The politics of sound

Few could have predicted in the early 1970s that the introduction of the Dolby noise reduction system was to spearhead a true revolution in the way film sound is created, recorded, reproduced and received by an audience. Thirty years on, it is possible to begin to map the key developments that have given rise to the Dolby era of sound in Hollywood cinema, as I hope this study has proved. Indeed, in this final chapter I would like to reflect briefly on what has arisen out of the evidence so far examined and highlight the aforementioned key features.

The tide of technological improvements that has characterised the development of the Dolby era since Dolby's arrival on the scene is one such key feature. This has been characterised by three aspects: continuity, stability and visibility. The introduction of the Dolby noise reduction system in 1971 ignited a succession of technological developments whose momentum has not yet shown signs of a slowdown. This element of continuous change has been characterised by a remarkable ability to identify new markets and possibilities. Dolby's latest ventures into digital broadcasting, the computer world (Dolby NET) and personal stereos (Dolby Headphone) offer some evidence of this apparently relentless growth, as well as provide clues as to where the Dolby era might be headed next in terms sound technology development.[1] An equally notable level of stability has matched this element of continuous development. Sound as a business venture has enjoyed an unprecedented period of stability and expansion in the Dolby era. This has not just been the case for Dolby Laboratories. Sound projects such as Lucasfilm's THX sound system, and the SDDS and DTS sound systems, have all proven to be extremely successful ventures, both in the cinema and home market (with the exception of

Sony's SDDS, all the sound systems mentioned are available to consumers in some form or other). Whereas in the past periods of technological innovation and financial success were often short-lived, the Dolby era is now in its fourth decade of expansion. Finally, this technological prowess has been very visible. The myriad of acronyms, logos and symbols that have become familiar to audience of Hollywood cinema worldwide is the tangible presence of these developments. The names Dolby (in all its incarnations), THX, DTS and SDDS, the double-D logo, the trailers that accompany these systems, their presence on film posters, their availability on all kind of consumer products (from videocassettes to DVDs, and from TV sets to home cinema processor) have contributed to making this revolution very visible as well as audible. Indeed, since over a billion products bearing the Dolby name and logo have been sold across the world, the suggestion that the name Dolby is today one of the most recognisable brand names in the world is not as implausible as it might seem.

The impact that technology has had on filmmakers has also been a defining factor in the Dolby era. This has been particularly true in terms of creative opportunities, filmmaking practices, and in the many ways in which this fertile situation has helped redefine professional figures. The dissociation of the terms 'mono' and 'optical sound' has been a key factor in providing filmmakers with new creative opportunities. The possibility to employ stereophonic sound, a wider frequency range and an ever-increasing dynamic range on conventional 35 mm optical prints has freed filmmakers from the old constraining choice of magnetic stereo vs. mono optical. This has characterised the Dolby era as one where filmmakers' confidence and ingenuity in employing sound is less hampered by technical and financial constraints than in the pre-Dolby period. Multi-channel soundtracks have become the norm rather than the domain of a few expensive films, and improved conditions of reproduction in theatres have helped create a sense of confidence in the possibility of using sound innovatively and effectively. In many ways, this newly found confidence is mirrored by the redefinition of professional figures. When Walter Murch and Ben Burtt begun employing terms such as 'sound designer' or 'sound montage', the attempt was to shift the focus from sound people as 'technicians' to sound people as 'creative' figures, both in political and creative terms. Many sound men and women, from Murch and Burtt to Rydstrom and

Davies, have had their work recognised in ways that past creators of sound never achieved. Moreover, their opinions have been heard and written about in record numbers, and their contribution to movies recognised in many ways. Despite continuing problems with both traditional academic accounts of filmmaking and entrenched views of the role of sound amongst filmmakers themselves, this new 'status' for sound has also marked a substantial increase in numeric terms of people involved in the making of a soundtrack. From sound mixers (often several for each of the three main categories: sound effects, dialogue and music) to foley artists, from re-recording mixers to music supervisors and composers, and from supervising sound editors to sound designers, the number of sound people involved in any given film has at times reached the size of a small army.[2]

All these changes have inevitably had consequences in terms of filmmaking practices. Although this is one of the areas that suffers most from the inevitable variations in practice that characterise different post-production facilities, the evident increase in number and status of sound people has meant that some of them are now able to get involved in pre-production and have a say in some key early decisions that are made at planning stage. This is still limited to a relatively small group of established, 'elite' sound people, but the emphasis on collaboration is what most sound people stress as potentially one of the defining factors of future stages of the Dolby era. Increasing political status might lead to greater collaboration between different sound departments (namely post-production sound and music) as well as different areas of filmmaking (in particular, choices in terms of scriptwriting, directing and editing that might later impact on sound). In this sense, the rise during the Dolby era of several new post-production facilities, such as Skywalker Sound (San Francisco),[3] Soundstorm (Los Angeles),[4] and Sound One (New York),[5] have provided the technological and creative opportunities for the new ranks of sound people to experiment and develop their craft. Indeed, at least in the case of Lucasfilm's Skywalker Sound, now a company in its own right, sound people have been in a position to influence directly the development of future technologies, as Gary Rydstrom's role in the development of Dolby's latest sound system, Dolby EX, demonstrates.[6] The period immediately preceding the success that Dolby was to enjoy with the release of *Star Wars* was not devoid of sound experimentation. Indeed, it exhibited clear signs of premonition in terms of what was to come. Some of the key sound people that would change the sound of Hollywood films were already at work. In particular, directors such as William Friedkin (*The French Connection* and *The Exorcist*), Francis Ford Coppola (*The Conversation* and *The Godfather*), George Lucas (*THX 1138* and *American Graffiti*), Robert Altman (*McCabe and Mrs Miller* and *Nashville*) and Steven Spielberg (*Duel* and *Jaws*) showed a remarkable level of sophistication in the early 1970s. Crucially they all benefited from being able to employ the skills and creativity of a new generation of filmmakers, such as sound designer Walter Murch, production sound mixer Chris Newman, sound re-recordist Richard Portman, and sound re-recordist Robert Hoyt. However, despite their unquestionable desire to explore sound in new terms – Murch, for instance, approached sound from a *musique concrète* perspective – the technological limitations that I have outlined above hindered aesthetic progress substantially.

The aforementioned developments in both technological and creative terms explain, partly at least, the relevance of a further defining factor in the Dolby era, namely the development of a new kind of relationship between audiences and film sound. This primarily revolves around three core aspects: changes in cinema architecture, the rise of a 'new' audience, and the home-cinema dimension. None of these is merely a direct consequence of the introduction of Dolby or any other sound technologies, but they have become inextricably linked since their meeting at a fortunate historical crossroad in the 1970s. The development of mall cinemas and the demise of old movie palaces created fertile ground for new developments to be adopted. Issues such as sound spillage from adjacent theatres, unwanted echoes, projector noise and other noise contributing factors (such as air conditioning and heating), speakers quality and theatre equalisation have all been addressed since the 1970s in an attempt to improve sound quality in the 'B chain' and raise it to approximate that of the 'A chain'. The development by Lucasfilm of the THX programme is perhaps the most enduring example of this drive for sound quality that has characterised cinema architecture and film reproduction in the Dolby era.[7] Ultimately, the demands on cinema acoustics that sound technology has placed on theatres have forced a fundamental rethink of the importance of sound in determining the way cinemas are built. The adoption by the Academy of new quality standards for sound reproduction, following Dolby's specifications, has been in this sense instrumental in removing cinemas from the time warp they had drifted into towards the late 1960s and propelling them into today's 'sonic playgrounds'. These drastically improved conditions of reproduction in theatres have arguably gone a long way in matching audience expectations as to what 'good sound' ought to sound like. As I have outlined earlier, filmmakers and innovators of the Dolby era directly addressed the rise of new aural expectations born out of the revolutionary decade, in aural terms, that was the 1960s.

In this sense, the relationship between Dolby, new technologies, emerging sound figures and the new generation of filmmakers (such as Lucas, Spielberg, Scorsese, Cimino, Kaufman and Coppola) that established itself as a dominant group in the late 1970s, is a further defining feature of the period I have investigated. Most noticeably, the industry's desire to pursue this relationship aggressively is very 'visible'. Perhaps this is best exemplified by the ways in which audiences are directly addressed as 'listeners' through film trailers of the various sound systems, and cinema advertisements emphasising which sound system theatre 'x' can boast. In this sense, the most important and visible aspect of this relationship is undoubtedly the home-cinema dimension. As I mentioned earlier, sales figures for Dolby-licensed products leave no doubt as to the pervasiveness of the name that symbolises the Dolby era. From television sets to computers, and from video recorders to DVD players, consumers have grown accustomed to good-quality sound in their home. The direct marketing of cinema sound systems to home audiences is further evidence of how this new kind of relationship between audiences of Hollywood cinema and sound has been carefully nurtured. Now your living room can be THX-certified!

Finally, the amount of institutional recognition of the importance that film sound has attained since the early 1970s is a further area that has helped define the Dolby era. Two aspects in particular are relevant here, namely the increase in academic attention devoted to sound, and the film industry's embracing of Dolby's developments. The development of a sizeable film sound scholarship during the Dolby era and the rise of the 'novel literature of sound' have kickstarted a transformation in the way film sound is regarded by academics and scholars the consequences of which have not yet fully matured, but that has the potential to be a defining feature of future scholarship in film studies. Similarly, the industry's initial reluctance to accept Dolby's new paradigm for sound quality has given way to a seemingly unassailable position of strength for Dolby where sound quality is concerned. Key figures within the Dolby organisation, such as Ray Dolby and Ioan Allen, have received many awards including Oscars for their contribution to the improvement of the art of film sound. Dolby's suggested parameters for theatre architecture have replaced the old Academy standards and are now codified (the 'X-curve') in US and international standards from the SMPTE and the ISO. All major studios now have a 'digital-only' release policy for their films, and they have all invested heavily in upgrading their sound facilities.

The significance of the Dolby era arises from reflecting on the developments that I have just outlined above in all their implications, both for the industry and for academia. When considering the size and scope of the changes that have taken place in the period that I have investigated, it is possible to state confidently that these have affected the whole of the film industry. The development of new sound technology, its adoption by filmmakers, the improvements in cinema architecture and film reproduction that followed, and the level of audience engagement with Hollywood movies paint a picture that is a far cry from its pre-Dolby times. It is in this sense of meaningful, sustained and pervasive development that the term 'era' can, and indeed need, be employed. The demarcation line between what Hollywood cinema was and what it is now, in all its aspects, appears to have been affected by film sound in a substantial and fundamental manner. Similarly, cinema as an object of study cannot delay much further the recognition of the central role that sound can play. The Dolby era and its legacy have provided scholars and critics with a wealth of opportunities to further their knowledge of and about the cinema, just as it has empowered filmmakers to advance their creativity. The questions that arise from established views of sound in movies are not simply relevant to sound; they are central to film studies as a whole. The answers theorists have given in the past to questions about the role and aesthetic potential of sound have shaped film studies both as an academic discipline and as a subject of general interest. However incisive and influential those past accounts of film might have been, the need for a re-examination of some core areas of film sound in light of the impact that the latter has had since the 1970s would now appear to be less a matter of personal choice and more one of intellectual integrity. Every major area of investigation has been affected, much as in the case of the film industry. The place of technology in filmmaking, the creative input that the makers of sound have on a movie, the role that sound plays in films, the relationship between audiences and cinema, the nature of central concerns such as genre, audiences, representation, auteurism, and textual analysis: all these areas would benefit substantially from an engagement with sound that went beyond harmful generalisations and indefensible subordinations. Sound matters.

Notes

1 More information on Dolby E, Dolby NET and Dolby Headphone can be found at www.dolby.com (accessed 30 August 2003).
2 In big-budget movies such as *Speed* and *The Fugitive* the number of sound men and women involved in the creation of a soundtrack can often reach the forty mark in post-production alone.
3 Official web site available at www.skysound.com (accessed 1 March 2003).
4 Official web site available at www.soundstorm.com (accessed 1 March 2003).
5 Official web site available at www.soundone.com (accessed 1 March 2003).
6 Dolby and Lucasfilm openly recognise Rydstrom's role in developing EX in their literature: see www.dolby.com/movies/interview_starwars. html (accessed 1 September 2002).
7 The THX programme is arguably the most comprehensive attempt at approximating B-chain reproduction to A-chain quality. In other words, it is an attempt to ensure that audiences hear what filmmakers heard when the film was made and not a sub-standard version of it. For more information, see the official THX site at www.thx.com (accessed 1 March 2003).

Appendices

Appendix 1

The look of Dolby

The success of Dolby technologies over the years has been marked by a remarkable degree of visibility on movie posters, film lobbies, movie prints and more recently, video cassettes, laserdiscs and DVDs. Indeed, Dolby's 'double-D' logo is one of the most enduring symbols of the Dolby era.[1] The official documentation produced by Dolby Labs that specifies which logos need to be used and in what occasion testifies to Dolby's desire to provide continuity by employing the same company image logo for over 30 years, as well as establishing the Dolby logo as a 'prestige' logo easily recognisable around the world.[2]

As the illustrations on the next few pages demonstrate, continuity has been the overarching concern in relation to the look and 'feel' of the various Dolby logos employed to promote the various sound systems and technologies over the years.

The following illustrations are part of Dolby's official artwork and document the 'development' of the look of Dolby since the 1970s.

Notes

1 The name Dolby, the Double-D logo and all other artwork appearing in this book are under copyright and cannot be reproduced without the explicit written consent of Dolby Laboratories.
2 Available at www.dolby.com/tm/info/AdPromoGuidelines.pdf (accessed 1 November 2002).

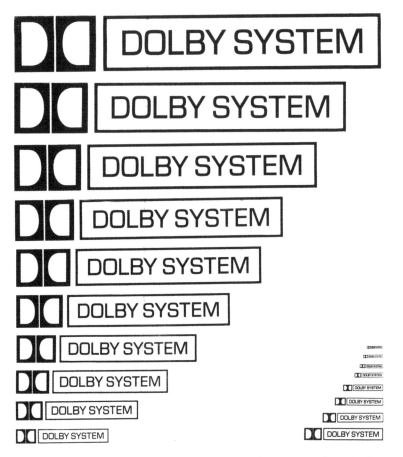

Figure 1 Dolby logos, 1970s, used for professional and consumer noise reduction equipment, and encoded consumer cassettes
Dolby and the double-D symbol are trade marks of Dolby Laboratories

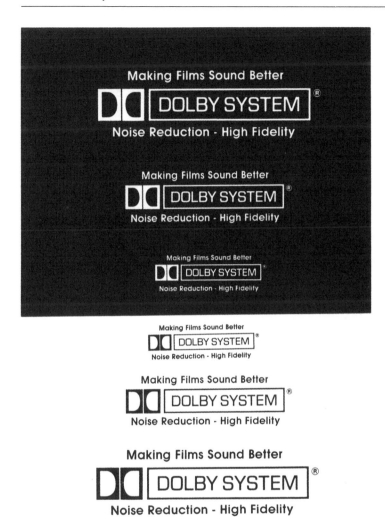

Figure 2 Dolby logos, 1970s/1980s, used, for example, on *Star Wars*, 1977
Dolby and the double-D symbol are trade marks of Dolby Laboratories

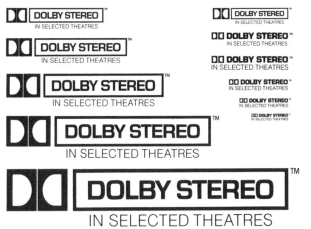

Figure 3 Dolby logos, film logos through the late 1970s and through the 1980s
Dolby and the double-D symbol are trade marks of Dolby Laboratories

Figure 4 Dolby logos, 1980s, used on professional noise reduction equipment
Dolby and the double-D symbol are trade marks of Dolby Laboratories

Figure 5 Dolby logos, 1990s, used for consumer video applications
Dolby and the double-D symbol are trade marks of Dolby Laboratories

Figure 6 Dolby logos, 1990s, first used for *Star Wars Episode I – The Phantom Menace* in 1999
Dolby and the double-D symbol are trade marks of Dolby Laboratories

Figure 7 In Dolby Stereo! Northpoint Theatre, San Francisco, 1979

Appendix 2

Academy Curve and X-curve comparison

The diagram below shows clearly the limiting impact that the Academy Curve had on pre-Dolby movies with its curtailing of both low and high frequencies. In particular, notice how the curve dips in both sections and that the frequency range it covers near 0 db (roughly 150 kHz to 3 kHz) is little better than conventional telephone-quality sound. Dolby's X-curve, on the other hand, covers a much greater range and with even power distribution.

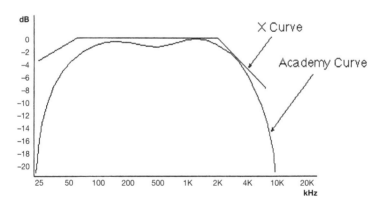

Source: www.editorsguild.com/newsletter/sepOct01/ioan_allen_one.html (accessed 10 December 2002).

Bibliography

Adair, Gilbert (ed.), *Movies* (London and New York: Penguin, 1999)

Allen, Ioan, 'The Dolby Sound System for Recording *Star Wars*', *American Cinematographer* (Vol. 58, Issue 6, July 1977)

Allen, Robert and Gomery, Douglas, *Film History – Theory and Practice* (New York: Alfred A. Knopf, 1985)

Altman, Rick (ed.), *Sound Theory, Sound Practice* (London and New York: Routledge, 1992)

Altman, Rick, *The American Film Musical* (Bloomington and Indianapolis: Indiana University Press, 1987)

Altman, Rick (ed.), *Cinema/Sound*, special issue on sound of *Yale French Studies* (Vol. 60, 1980)

Altman, Rick, '24-Track Narrative? Robert Altman's *Nashville*', *Cinema* (Vol. 5, Issue 1.3, 1991)

Altman, Rick, 'The Sound of Sound – A Brief History of the Reproduction of Sound in Movie Theaters', *Cinéaste* (Vol. 21, Issue 1–2, 1995) – supplement 'Sound and Music in the Movies', pp. 68–71

Arick, Michael, 'In Stereo! The Sound of Money', *Sight & Sound* (Vol. 57, winter 1987–88)

Armes, Roy, 'Entendre, c'est comprendre: In Defence of Sound Reproduction', *Screen* (Vol. 29, Issue 2, spring 1988), pp. 8–22

Arnheim, Rudolph, *Film* (London: Faber & Faber, 1933)

Arnheim, Rudolph, *Film as Art* (Berkeley, Los Angeles and London: University of California Press, 1971)

Austin, Bruce, *Immediate Seating – A Look at Movie Audiences* (Belmont, CA: Wadsworth Publishing Company, 1989)

Balasz, Bela, *Theory of Film* (New York: Arno Press and The New York Times, 1972 [1952])

Balio, Tino, *The American Film Industry* (Madison: University of Wisconsin Press, 1976)

Bazin, André, *What is Cinema?* (Berkeley, Los Angeles and London: University of California Press, 1967)

Beaugrand, Claude, 'Entendre l'arbre qui pousse', *24 Images* (Issue 60, spring 1992), pp. 32–33

Berman, Robert, *Fade In: The Screenwriting Process* (Studio City, CA: Michael Wiese, 1998)

Biondo, Giovanni and Sacchi, Enrico, *Riproduzione Sonora Hi-Fi* (Milano: Hoepli, 1984)

Biskind, Peter, *Easy Riders, Raging Bulls* (New York: Simon & Schuster, 1998)

Blake, Larry, 'Mixing Techniques for Dolby Stereo Film and Video Releases', *Recording Engineer/Producer* (June 1985), pp. 94–105

Blocker, John, 'Synthesised Sound for Brainstorm', *American Cinematographer* (Vol. 65, Issue 5, May 1984), pp. 95–98.

Bobrow, Andrew C., 'The Art of the Soundman: An Interview with Christopher Newman', *Filmmakers Newsletter* (Vol. 7, Issue 7, May 1974), pp. 24–25.

Bordwell, David, *Making Meaning – Inference and Rhetoric in the Interpretation of Cinema* (Cambridge, MA, and London: Harvard University Press, 1989)

Bordwell, David, *Narration in the Fiction Film* (Madison: University of Wisconsin Press, 1985)

Bordwell, David and Carroll, Noel (eds.), *Post Theory – Reconstructing Film Studies* (Madison and London: University of Wisconsin Press, 1996)

Bordwell, David and Thompson, Kristin, *Film Art – An Introduction* (New York: McGraw-Hill, 1993)

Bordwell, David and Thompson, Kristin, *Film History – An Introduction* (New York: McGraw-Hill, 1994)

Bordwell, David, Steiger, Janet and Thompson, Kristin, *The Classical Hollywood Cinema* (New York: Columbia University Press, 1985)

Bottomore, Stephen, 'An International Survey of Sound Effects in Early Cinema', *Film History* (Vol. 11, Issue 4, 1999), pp. 485–498

Branston, Gill, *Cinema and Cultural Modernity* (Buckingham, and Philadelphia, PA: Open University Press, 2000)

Buckland, Warren, *Teach Yourself Film Studies* (London: Hodder & Stoughton, 1998)

Burlingate Jon and Crowous, Gary, 'Music at the Service of Cinema – An Interview with Ennio Morricone', *Cinéaste* (Vol. 21, Issue 1–2, 1995) – supplement 'Sound and Music in the Movies', pp. 76–80

Carroll, Peter and Noble, David, *The Free and the Unfree – A New History of the United States* (London and New York: Penguin, 1988)

Caughie, John, *Theories of Authorship* (London and New York: Routledge, 2001)

Chernoff, Scott, 'Interview with John Williams', *Star Wars – The Official Magazine* (Issue 21, July/August 1999), pp. 24–28

Chion, Michel, *Audio-Vision – Sound on Screen* (New York: Columbia University Press, 1990)

Chion, Michel, *The Voice in the Cinema* (New York: Columbia University Press, 1998)

Chion, Michel, 'Revolution douce ... et dure stagnation', *Cahiers du Cinéma* (Issue 398, July/August 1987), p. 28

Church-Gibson, Pamela and Hill, John (eds.), *The Oxford Guide to Film Studies* (Oxford and New York: Oxford University Press, 1998)

Coffey, John, 'An Open Letter from Your Sound Department', available at: www.soundspeedmovie.com/resources/articles/coffey/openletter.html (accessed 1 September 2002)

Cook, Pam, *The Cinema Book* (London: British Film Institute, 1999)

Cowie, Peter, *The Apocalypse Now Book* (London and New York: Faber & Faber, 2000)

Cowie, Peter, *The Godfather Book* (London and New York: Faber & Faber, 1998)

Darby, Williams and DuBois, Jack, *American Film Music* (Jefferson, NC, and London: McFarland and Company, 1990)

De Palma, Brian, 'The Making of *The Conversation*: An Interview with Francis Ford Coppola', *Filmmakers Newsletter* (Vol. 7, Issue 7, May 1974), pp. 30–34

Ellis, John, *Visible Fictions* (London and New York: Routledge & Kegan Paul, 1982)

Elsaesser, Thomas and Buckland, Warren, *Studying Contemporary American Film – A Guide to Film Analysis* (London: Arnold, 2002)

Foner, Eric, *The History of American Freedom* (New York: Papermac, 2000)

Gentry, Richard, 'Alan Splet and Sound Effects for *Dune*', *American Cinematographer* (Vol. 65, Issue 11, December 1984), pp. 62–72

Gledhill, Christine and Williams, Linda (eds.), *Reinventing Film Studies* (London: Arnold, 2000)

Gomery, Douglas, 'Problems in Film History: How Fox Innovated Sound', *Quarterly Review of Film Studies* (Vol. 1, Issue 3, August 1976), pp. 315–330

Gomery, Douglas, 'The Coming of Sound: Technological Change in the American Film Industry', in John Belton and Elisabeth Weis (eds.), *Film Sound: Theory and Practice* (New York: Columbia University Press, 1985), pp. 5–24

Gorbman, Claudia, *Unheard Melodies: Narrative Film Music* (Bloomington and Indianapolis: Indiana University Press, 1987)

Gorbman, Claudia, 'Film Music', in P. Church Gibson and J. Hill (eds.), *The Oxford Guide to Film Studies* (Oxford: Oxford University Press, 1998), pp. 43–50

Gorbman, Claudia, 'The State of Film Music Criticism', *Cinéaste* (Vol. 21, Issue 1–2, 1995) – supplement 'Sound and Music in the Movies', pp. 72–75

Handzo, Stephen, 'The Golden Age of Film Music', *Cinéaste* (Vol. 21, Issue 1–2, 1995) – supplement 'Sound and Music in the Movies', pp. 46–55

Hayward, Susan, *Cinema Studies – The Key Concepts* (London: Routledge, 2000)

Hilliard, John K., 'Loudspeakers and Amplifiers for Use With Stereophonic Reproduction in the Theater', available at: www.widescreenmuseum. com/widescreen/53stereo.htm (accessed 14 January 2004)

Hillier, Jim, *The New Hollywood* (London: Studio Vista, 1992)

Hollows, Joanne, Jancovich, Mark and Hutchings, Peter (eds.), *The Film Studies Reader* (London: Arnold, 2000)

Holman, Tomlinson, *5.1 Surround Sound: Up and Running* (Woburn, MA: Focal Press, 1999)

Holman, Tomlinson, *Sound for Film and Television* (Woburn, MA: Focal Press, 2001)

Karney, Robin (ed.), *Chronicle of the Cinema* (London and New York: Dorling Kindersley, 1995)

Katz, Joy, 'In Conversation with Walter Murch', *Parnassus: Poetry in Review (The Movie Issue)* (Vol. 22, Issue 1/2,), pp. 124–153

Kawin, Bruce, *How Movies Work* (Berkeley, Los Angeles and London: University of California Press, 1992)

Kozloff, Sarah, *Overhearing Film Dialogue* (Berkeley, Los Angeles and London: University of California Press, 2000)

Lacan, Jacques, 'The Mirror Stage as Formative Function of the I', in Jacques Lacan, *Ecrits: A Selection* (London: Tavistock Publications, 1977)

Lambert, Mel, 'Freeze Frame', *Studio Sound Magazine* available at: www.soundstorm.com: click on news > archive to find the article.

La Polla, Franco, 'Steven Spielberg', *Il castoro cinema* (Issue 99, May/June 1982)

Lastra, James, *Sound Technology and the American Cinema* (New York: Columbia niversity Press, 2000)

LeBlanc, Sydney, *20th Century American Architecture* (New York: Watson-Guptill Publications, 1996)

Levin, Tom, 'The Acoustic Dimension: Notes on Cinema Sound', *Screen* (Vol. 25, Issue 3, May–June 1984)

LoBrutto, Vincent, *By Design: Interviews with Film Production Designers* (New York and London: Greenwood Press, 1992)

LoBrutto, Vincent, *Selected Takes: Film Editors in Editing* (New York and London: Greenwood Press, 1991)

LoBrutto, Vincent, *Sound-on-Film – Interviews with Creators of Film Sound* (Westport, CT, and London: Praeger, 1994)

Lovell, Alan and Kramer, Peter, *Screen Acting as Art and Performance* (London and New York: Routledge, 1999)

Maltby, Richard and Craven, Ian, *Hollywood Cinema* (Oxford, and Cambridge, MA: Blackwell, 1995)

Mancini, Mark, 'As Time Warps By', *Film Comment* (Vol. 23, Issue 5, September/October 1987), pp. 2–6.

Mancini, Mark, 'Sound Thinking', *Film Comment* (Vol. 19, Issue 6, November/December 1983)

Marwick, Arthur, *The Sixties* (Oxford and New York: Oxford University Press, 1998)

McQuail, Denis, *Mass Communication Theory* (London: Sage, 1994)

Monaco, James, *How to Read a Film* (Oxford and New York: Oxford University Press, 2000)

Morgan, Robert, *Modern Times* (Englewood Cliffs, NJ: Prentice Hall, 1994)

Mueder Eaton, Marcia, *Basic Issues in Aesthetics* (Belmont, CA: Wadsworth Publishing Company, 1988)

Mulvey, Laura, 'Visual Pleasure and Narrative Cinema', *Screen* (Vol. 16, Issue 3, autumn 1975)

Mulvey, Laura, 'Afterthoughts on "Visual Pleasure and Narrative Cinema" inspired by *Duel in the Sun*', *Framework* (Issue 15/16/17, summer 1981)

Murch, Muriel, 'Conversation with Walter Murch and Michael Ondaatje', in John Boorman and Walter Donohue (eds.), *Projections 8 – Filmmakers on Film-making* (London: Faber & Faber, 1998), pp. 311–326

Murch, Walter, *Dense Clarity, Clear Density*, available at: www.ps1.org/cut/volume/murch.html (accessed 1 September 2002)

Neale, Steve, *Cinema and Technology: Image, Sound, Colour* (London: British Film Institute, 1985)

Neale, Steve, 'Hollywood Corner', *Framework* (Issue 19, 1982), p. 37

Neale, Steve and Smith, Murray (eds.), *Contemporary Hollywood Cinema* (London and New York: Routledge, 1998)

Nelmes, Jill (ed.), *Introduction to Film Studies* (London and New York: Routledge, 1996)

Pasquariello, Nicholas and Pepper, C., 'Basic Instinct', *American Cinematographer* (Vol. 73, Issue 4, April 1992), pp. 44–55

Perkins, Victor, *Film as Film* (London and New York: Penguin, 1972)

Phillips, William H., *Film: An Introduction* (Basingstoke: Palgrave Macmillan, 2002)

Rockwell, John, *All American Music – Composition in the Late Twentieth Century* (London: Kahn & Averill, 1985)

Salt, Barry, *Film Style and Technology: History and Analysis* (London: Starword, 1983)

Schreger, Charles, 'The Second Coming of Sound', *Film Comment* (Vol. 14, Issue 5, 1978)

Scotland, John, *The Talkies* (London: 1930)

Seger, Linda and Whetmore, Edward Jay, *From Script to Screen – The Collaborative Art of Filmmaking* (New York: Henry Holt and Company, 1994)

Serafine, Frank, 'Creating the Undersea Sounds of Red October', *American Cinematographer* (Vol. 71, Issue 9, September 1990)

Serafine, Frank, 'The New Motion Picture Sound', *American Cinematographer* (Vol. 61, Issue 8, August 1980)

Sergi, Gianluca, 'A Cry in the Dark: The Role of Postclassical Film Sound', in Steve Neale and Murray Smith (eds.), *Contemporary Hollywood Cinema* (London and New York: Routledge, 1998), pp. 156–165. Available also in Graeme Turner (ed.), *The Film Cultures Reader* (London and New York: Routledge, 2002), pp. 107–114

Sergi, Gianluca, *The Use of the Voice in Film*, in Laura Vichi (ed.), *The Visible Man* (Udine: Forum Press, 2002)

Sergi, Gianluca, 'The Hollywood Sonic Playground: The Spectator as Listener', in Richard Maltby and Melvyn Stokes (eds.), *Hollywood Spectatorship* (London: British Film Institute, 2001), pp. 121–131.

Sergi, Gianluca, 'Actors and the Sound Gang', in Peter Kramer and Alan Lovell (eds.), *Screen Acting as Art and Performance* (London and New York: Routledge, 1999), pp. 126–137.

Sergi, Gianluca, 'Tales of the Silent Blast: *Star Wars* and Sound', *Journal of Popular Film and Television* (Vol. 26, Issue 1, spring 1998)

Sharples, Winston, 'A Selected and Annotated Bibliography of Books and Articles on Music in the Cinema', *Cinema Journal* (Vol. 17, Issue 2, spring 1978)

Sharples, Winston, 'The Aesthetics of Film Sound', *Filmmakers Newsletter* (Vol. 8, Issue 5, March 1975)

Shilling, Edward, 'Digital Sound for Film and Video, *American Cinematographer* (Vol. 65, Issue 11, December 1984)

Smith, Jeff, *The Sounds of Commerce – Marketing Popular Film Music* (New York: Columbia University Press, 1998)

Sonnenschein, David, *Sound Design – The Expressive Power of Music, Voice and Sound Effects in Cinema* (Studio City, CA: Michael Wiese, 2001)

Sontag, Susan, *Against Interpretation* (London: Vintage, 1994)

Stokes, Melvyn and Maltby, Richard (eds.), *Hollywood Spectatorship – Changing Perspectives of Cinema Audiences* (London: British Film Institute, 2001)

Sturmahn, Larry, 'The Art of the Sound Editor: An Interview with Walter Murch', *Filmmakers Newsletter* (Vol. 8, Issue 2, December 1974)

Thom, Randy, 'Designing a Movie for Sound', available at www.filmsound.org/articles/designing_for_sound.htm (accessed 1 September 2002)

Thom, Randy, 'Mixing A Different Box of Chocolates – A Few Notes on Forrest Gump', available at www.filmsound.org/randythom/forrest.htm (accessed 20 September 2002)

Turner, Graeme (ed.), *The Film Cultures Reader* (London and New York: Routledge, 2002)

Various, special issue on film sound of *Film Comment* (Vol. 24, Issue 5, September–October 1978)

Vichi, Laura (ed.), *The Visible Man* (Udine: Forum, 2001)

Warner, Frank 'The Sounds of Silence and Things that go "Flash" in the Night', *American Cinematographer* (Vol. 59, Issue 1, January 1978)

Warner Sperling, Cass and Millner, Cork, *Hollywood Be Thy Name – The Warner Brothers Story* (Rockling, CA: Prima Publishing, 1994)

Webb, James E. 'Multi-Channel Dialogue and Effects Recording During Film Production', *American Cinematographer* (Vol. 60, Issue 4, April 1979)

Weis, Elisabeth, *The Silent Scream – Alfred Hitchcock's Soundtrack* (Rutherford, NJ: Fairleigh Dickinson University Press, 1982)

Weis, Elisabeth, 'Synch Tanks – The Art and Technique of Post-production Sound', *Cinéaste* (Vol. 21, Issue 1–2, 1995) – supplement 'Sound and Music in the Movies', pp. 56–61. Available also at: www.geocities.com /Hollywood/Academy/4394/sync.htm (accessed 1 October 2002)

Weis, Elisabeth, 'The Sound of One Wing Flapping', *Film Comment* (Vol. 14, Issue 5, 1978)

Weis, Elisabeth and Belton, John (eds.), *Film Sound: Theory and Practice* (New York: Columbia University Press, 1985)

Woodham, Jonathan, *Twentieth-Century Design* (Oxford and New York: Oxford University Press, 1997)

Wyver, John, *The Moving Image* (Oxford and New York: Blackwell and British Film Institute, 1989)

Young, John, 'Sound Revolution', *Hollywood Reporter* (22 June 1993)

Other Internet sources

Digital Theater Sound (DTS) official site, available at www.dtsonline.com

Dolby Laboratories official site, available at www.dolby.com

Filmsound.org (online articles on film sound), available at www.filmsound. org

Lucasfilm THX official site, available at www.thx.com

Skywalker Sound official site, available at www.skysound.com

Sony Dynamic Digital Sound (SDDS) official site, available at www.sdds.com

Sound One official site available at www.soundone.com

Soundstorm official site, available at www.soundstorm.com

The Widescreen Museum (online articles on widescreen processes and stereophonic sound), available at www.widescreenmuseum.com

Index

Guildford College
Learning Resource Centre
Please return on or before the last date shown.
No further issues or renewals if any items are overdue.
"7 Day" loans are **NOT** renewable.

Class: _778.5344 SER_

Title: _The Dolby Era_

Author: _Sergi, G_